PLEASE DON'T TELL MY PARENTS

DAWSON McALLISTER

WORD PUBLISHING

Dallas · London · Vancouver · Melbourne

Please Don't Tell My Parents

The letters reproduced in this publication are drawn from actual letters addressed to Dawson McAllister. The names and details, however, have been changed to preserve the privacy of the individuals involved.

Unless otherwise indicated, all Scripture quotations in this book are from the Holy Bible, New Century Version, Copyright © 1987, 1988, 1991 by Word Publishing, Dallas, Texas. Used by permission.

Other Scripture quotations are from the following sources:

The Holy Bible, New International Version, NIV, Copyright © 1973, 1978, 1984 by International Bible Society. Used by permission of Zondervan Publishing House.

The Living Bible, TLB, Copyright © 1971 by Tyndale House Publishers, Wheaton, Illinois. Used by permission.

The New American Standard Bible, NASB, Copyright © 1960, 1962, 1963, 1968, 1971, 1972, 1973, 1975, 1977 by The Lockman Foundation, La Habra, California. Used by permission.

Library of Congress Cataloging-in-Publication Data:

McAllister, Dawson
    Please don't tell my parents / Dawson McAllister.
      p. cm.
    Summary: Uses a Christian perspective to address such adolescent problems as dysfunctional homes, suicide, sex, and substance abuse.
    ISBN 0–8499–3311–0
    1. Teenagers–Conduct of life. 2. Teenagers—Religious life.
[1. Conduct of life. 2. Christian life.] I. Title.
BJ1661.M27   1992
248.8'3—dc20   92–10665
                                                  CIP
                                                  AC

3 4 5 9   LB   9 8 7 6 5 4 3

Printed in the United States of America

Contents

Introduction

Will the Real American Teenager Please Stand Up?

FOR OVER TWENTY YEARS I'VE TALKED TO STUDENTS ACROSS AMERICA ABOUT THE REALITY OF JESUS CHRIST. I have seen all kinds of teenagers, from drug dealers and gang members to the most committed Christian teenagers. I have listened to them, and they have trusted me. I have learned that they are not afraid of the truth. Like all of us, teens want compassion and sympathy for their hurts and struggles. But they also want answers—honest, straight-ahead, no-punches-pulled answers.

Many students write me letters. I feel honored when these students pour out their hearts to me. I like to receive their letters because they provide a much clearer picture of what's really going on inside of them. However, these letters also leave me feeling saddened and deeply concerned for the future of America's teenagers. I have come to two painful and somewhat frightening conclusions.

First, today's teenagers have more cars, more clothes, more jobs, and more money than any other generation of teenagers. On the surface, this makes most of them look as if they are happy and have it all together. But underneath there are many who are in tremendous emotional and spiritual pain. There are

8

millions who feel unloved, unneeded, and unimportant.
The second conclusion is, in some ways, more
frightening. Today there are almost as many Christian
teenagers struggling as non-Christian teenagers. Even
within the church, families have broken up and morals
have broken down at a horrendous rate. Students want
to believe in love and commitment. They want to believe that God is in control. Unfortunately, they are
often surrounded by so much failure and hypocrisy that
they lose hope.

We all know that it has never been easy to be a
teenager, but as we head toward the twenty-first century, I believe it's getting more difficult every day. Let
me illustrate what I am saying. The following two
letters came in the mail the same day. Note the remarkable differences between them.

Dear Dawson,

I have enclosed $5 for use in your ministry of reaching
students. I know it is not much, but I'm going to ask my
friends to support your ministry as well. We will be taking
about twenty or so kids to your conference this weekend.
After this great weekend I'm sure some will want to support you in reaching other teens. Thank you for allowing the
Lord to minister to me through you. God bless you.

Your friend 'til Life,
Anne

Now, here is a committed teenage girl! She is a
leader. She gave $5 of her own money so that others will
be reached for Christ. She wants to get others in her
youth group to be involved, as well. She evidently loves

God greatly. She is the kind of girl any youth minister would want in his youth group. Now look at the second letter.

Dear Dawson,

I'm sixteen years old and I have an older brother. When I was between the ages of three and twelve, I was used by him for all imaginable purposes—and a few things that can not even be imagined. These memories were pretty much brainwashed out of my head because I just blacked them out—at least until a little over two years ago. Jim came back into my room. He was drunker than drunk. This was a day or two before I left on a mission trip with my youth group. I didn't sleep at all hardly until the trip. When I did sleep, my dreams would wake me up. I told my youth leader, who had me tell my pastor, who had me tell a police officer, who had me give a statement, who didn't do anything and weeks later said he couldn't because it had been too long since anything happened and I was in no immediate danger.

Still, I can't sleep at night. I miss an average of a day a week of school because I stay at home and try to sleep while my brother is at work. Like most other teens, I barely see my parents. Not much chance of me telling them. I know my mom already knows because she used to "catch us in the act." She never said anything. I'm totally stressed out because I don't sleep. I don't know what to do. I think I'm gonna crack soon. Within the past year I've met at least twenty people in the same situation I'm in and they all want advice. The only reason I have it as together as I do is because I have Jesus Christ. And a lot of the time I can look as though I'm doing great on the outside but be going crackers on the inside.

10

Please help me if ya can, I'm fixing to lose it I'm afraid. God bless.

Your friend 'til Life,
Anne

Did you notice how each letter was signed? Both used the phrase, "Your friend 'til Life, Anne." I looked carefully at the handwriting. Both letters were, indeed, written by the same person. I was overwhelmed by the incredible conflict that was taking place inside this girl. Anne #1 is a giver. She doesn't ask anything for herself, nor does she complain of her circumstances. She seems to be doing amazingly well. But Anne #2 is another story altogether. She is in serious trouble. For her, things are going downhill quickly. She is being used and abused and no one seems to care. Anne #1 enclosed a gift to help the students of America. Anne #2 enclosed a plea for help from a terrible world of abuse, fear, and sleepless nights. What a difference. On the outside, peace and tranquility, but on the inside, deep, dark inner struggles.

Whether you're a teenager or an adult, you need to ask yourself how many Annes you know. She might be your best friend. She might be your neighbor. This poor victim might even be your own daughter. How do you know she's not? How do you know that your best friend is not being sexually abused by her brothers or her father? How do you know that the person who sits next to you in English class is not going through tor-ment night after night? How do you know that your own children are safe from harm in a depraved world? I hope that you are as horrified as I am, because I am convinced that the Annes of this world are all around us.

So what can we do for a girl like Anne? Is there any hope? As Christians, we know there is. Absolutely! God is still in the business of healing lives. The Bible tells us:

He heals the brokenhearted and bandages their wounds.

Psalm 147:3

Somehow we must get the message of God's clear and unchanging truth to hurting and desperate students everywhere. They need to understand that God does, indeed, love them and that He can heal their deepest wounds. It is our job to bring God's powerful, all-healing love into their lives. This job will not be easy. It will be a tedious and painful process. Their heartbreak is so deep that few feel they can even tell their parents about it.

Several years ago a youth worker friend of mine was talking to me about the staggering growth in sexual abuse. He made a short, simple statement that I will never forget. He said, "You know, the problems of sexual abuse are not going to be solved by a youth group hay ride." I thought to myself, *How true that is.* Really helping teenagers is one of the most difficult things we will ever attempt. But if the next generation is to be won for Christ, we must do it.

This book has been written for several groups of people. First of all, it is written for hurting students. If you are a student who has deep needs, my prayer is that you'll be able to identify with some of the problems other students have shared in their letters. My hope is that my answers to them will also be answers to you. Don't give up. God has put this book in your hands for a reason. Read it, and then act on the advice that applies to your life.

12

This book is also written for anyone who cares about what is going in the world of the American student—a parent, a grandparent, a Sunday school teacher, a youth pastor, a teacher. No matter who you are, I believe you will be able to use the counsel in this book to reach out to needy students who God has brought into your life.

I am convinced that God has not given up on the American teenager. He is the answer to the deepest problems they face. So, come with me on this difficult, but necessary, journey into the needs and the heartbreak of kids. Together, let us find answers for them in the Bible, God's Word. And then let us be used by God to "heal the brokenhearted and bandage their wounds."

1

The Misuse of Sex

> "I don't want to lose him.
> I've broken up with him twice,
> but find myself alone."
> —Gloria

WHEN IT COMES TO SEX AND THE AMERICAN TEENAGER, our reactions are all over the place. Some people ignore it. Some people pretend it doesn't exist. Some people feel overwhelmed and helpless to do anything about it. And some people are convinced that it's simply inevitable. How do you feel about helping teenagers deal with their sexuality?

Let me tell you how I feel. Denial, hand wringing, and giving up are not answers; they're cop outs. The problem of the misuse of sex among American teenagers is both huge and deadly serious. We can't wish it away, and we can't afford to condone it. Here are some cold, hard statistics.

- By the time a student is a senior in high school, 72 percent of his or her classmates have had sex.

- On any given day, 44 percent of the teen population engages in sexual behavior.

- Only 21 percent of girls think premarital sex is a "bad idea" for everyone.

And what about Christian teenagers? Surveys show that their sexual activity is almost as great as that of their non-Christian friends.

16

Should we be surprised that sex is so big among teenagers, even Christian teenagers? I think not. As a society, we first tell our students not to have sex. Then we bombard them with sexual messages in advertising and entertainment, breaking down any morality we have managed to build up. Finally, we tell them that they are responsible if they practice safe sex by using condoms, as if that solves all the problems of the misuse of sex. What a set of mixed messages that is. At best, most teenagers are confused. At worst, they have no sense of sexual morality whatsoever.

Perhaps the worst injustice occurs when we fail to tell students about the emotional and spiritual consequences of premarital sex. We tell them how to avoid diseases and unwanted pregnancy, but we seldom tell them about the heartache, pain, and bitterness of "love" gone bad. We seldom talk about the deep wounds that come from giving your body away outside of the commitment and security of marriage. Think about this: When teenage girls are asked why they have sex, over half say they've been pressured into it. And 75 percent of all teens believe that peer pressure causes most students to have sex even if they'd rather wait.

God never intended for the American student to carry the burdens of guilt, low self-esteem, and the sense of rejection that come with the misuse of sex. Yet, He is in the business of healing the lives of those who are already carrying these burdens. This chapter contains letters from Gloria and Bobby, two students who have made the mistake of "going too far." Their pain is real. However, I hope you will focus in on the even greater reality of God's wise counsel and His healing love, which teaches us that we don't have to run from the problems of the misuse of sex. God's answers still have the power to work in today's teenage world.

A Letter from Gloria

Dear Dawson,

I've been sitting alone in my room for about two hours. My mind has been wandering and I found myself crying. What have I done? And how can I change? I went to your youth conference in Atlanta this year. It was great. But it seems like I'm drifting farther and farther away from God. I'm a Christian. But I've made some mistakes. I've been in a relationship with a guy for a year and a half. He's not a Christian. I invite him to church all the time, but he's always got an excuse. But then I found myself doing things I thought I'd never do. At first I had a dead set answer, NO, but I wasn't strong enough. Now I'm having sex. I don't want to. I listen to your tapes about sex, love and dating. But I'm too stupid to make decisions. I have a hard time making decisions. I don't want to lose him. I've broken up with him twice, but find myself alone. But he is the one I tell everything to. Again and again I ask God for forgiveness, but then I do it again. I feel trapped and don't know what to do. Do I like this guy enough to let him go? Will I have someone else ever again to be close to? I'm such a hypocrite. I love the Lord so much, but I keep hurting Him. Please write to me. Be my friend.

Dawson, this is how I feel:

Scared

Feel like I'm deceiving

Don't want to hide things from parents

I'm hurting myself

18

I feel alone
How can I get out of this?
I've lost my virginity
I miss you, God

Will you forgive me Lord?

I love my father

What will he think of me?

He holds me. I love him

I can tell him everything

What do I do?

Can I be pure again?

I need to know the Word
I've misled him

I think its wrong
I have no friends to talk to
He's the only one I have
I wish we could get right with
the Lord
Is he not destined to be yours,
Lord?
What will my parents think of
me?
I'm going to lose my parents'
respect
I feel I have someone when I'm
with him
Can we have a Christian rela-
tionship later?
He's not bringing me close to
you, Lord
Will my future husband have a
great love for me?
I'm a hypocrite
I feel alone

Gloria

Dear Gloria,

Thank you for your letter. I count it a privilege that you would pour out your heart to me about your boyfriend and your sexuality. I have read your letter over and over again. Your problems are not small ones, but they are not impossible either. Gloria, I am completely convinced that God has answers for you. These answers may be painful to accept, but in the end they will lead to healing and a new life.

I think that most of the hurts and needs you share in your letter are summed up in the questions you ask at the beginning of your letter: "What have I done and how can I change?" I will do my best to answer this question in this letter.

To answer your question, "What have I done?" we need to begin by looking at your situation. You started dating a non-Christian guy. After a while the relationship got physical. Eventually, you went "all the way" with him. You'd like to break up with him, but you can't bear the thought of being without him. On the one hand, having sex makes you feel loved and accepted. On the other hand, you feel real guilt knowing that you have sinned against God. You want to quit having sex with your boyfriend, but you can't seem to keep from doing it. You like the closeness with your boyfriend, but are agonizing over the feeling of distance that now exists between you and God. You keep asking God to forgive you, but then you give in again and start the pain and guilt all over. You have created a no-win situation for yourself that is tearing you apart.

Gloria, you ended your letter by writing a long list of your feelings. However, I don't think you really understand your deepest emotional and spiritual needs. So I want to challenge you to look more deeply at who you really are. I want you to be open to the painful truths about yourself that I am going to share.

I think that, down deep, you are terrified of being abandoned and alone with no one to love you. You verbalized these fears when you made such statements as: "I don't want to lose him. I've broken up with him twice, but find myself alone." "But he is the one I tell everything to." "Will I have someone else ever again to be close to?" "I feel alone, I have no friends to talk to." "I feel I have someone when I'm with him." "What do I do? I don't want to lose him," "Will my future husband have a great love for me?"

Underneath these fears is an even greater fear. It is the fear that God will not meet the deepest needs in your life. Because of this fear, you have decided to "play God." In other words, you have set out to meet your needs for love and acceptance without God. Now let's go back and figure out how all of these fears got you into this mess with your boyfriend.

After you met him, you became attracted to him, not only physically, but emotionally. Perhaps you felt more alive when you were with him. You sensed he was meeting a need in your life that had not been met before. But there was one small problem. Your boyfriend wasn't a Christian. Down deep, you knew you shouldn't get involved with him, but by this time you really felt you loved him. Now you had a very difficult choice to make: Obey God by breaking up with your non-Christian boyfriend, or ignore God and keep getting more heavily involved with your "new love." Put another way, you could let God fill your need for love and acceptance, or you could make the mistake of trying to meet it yourself. You came to the conclusion that your new love and the needs that you thought he was meeting were just too much to give up. To put it bluntly, you chose your non-Christian boyfriend over obeying God. You were so afraid of being alone that you couldn't bring yourself to end your romance, even though you knew it was destructive.

Gloria, I know that it was exciting when you began to date this guy. In the words of an old popular song,

"How can it be wrong when it feels so right?" But what you didn't realize is that he had his needs, too. Since he was a non-Christian, he couldn't turn to God to meet his needs. Nor could he turn to God to give him the self-control to say no to sex. Therefore, he turned to having sex with you. Let's face it, he had tremendous power over you. After all, he could break up at any time and leave you abandoned and alone. Thus, even though you said no for a while, the fear of his leaving you and of being alone was more than you could take. You had a decision to make: Do I give him my body or breakup with him? Do I trade sex for security, or do I obey God and refuse to give in? In the end, your need for love and acceptance from your boyfriend overshadowed your commitment to love and obey God. Yes, you said no for a while, but finally you gave your virginity away.

When you gave your body away to your boyfriend, I'm sure you had no idea how much having sex would affect your emotions. You experienced a feeling of closeness with him that you had not experienced with anyone else. You shared something so powerful, so sacred, that it all but overwhelmed you. But at the same time you felt tremendous guilt knowing that you had violated both your standards and God's standards concerning sex.

Now you find yourself in a double trap. If you break up with him you will lose that deep sense of closeness that you have achieved. You will find yourself having to face the fact that you have lost him and are now alone. But if you don't get out of this relationship, your life could be all but ruined. It's like you're balanced on a high wire where the slightest wind could blow you off to certain death. Gloria, we have to find a

22

way to get you out of this mess. We must answer your question, "How can I change?"

You have a big decision to make. Do you stay with your boyfriend, or do you leave him completely? This decision will not be an easy one. No matter what choice you make, you are going to hurt. There is no pain-free answer to your problem. The questions you have to ask yourself are, "What is the right thing to do?" and "What decision will give me hope?"

Before you make your decision, I want to help you clearly understand a few things. To begin with, I don't believe that your relationship with your non-Christian boyfriend is based on real love. Instead, I think it's based on several negative things. I think it's based on unmet needs and your confusion about how to meet those needs. I think it's based partly on selfishness. And I think it's based somewhat on fantasy. You're looking for real love. However, because of your confusion, your selfishness, and the fantasy that's playing in your mind, it's been almost impossible for you to realize that you have not had real love. You see, Gloria, real love comes from God because God is love. The Bible is clear on this. It says in 1 John 4:

> **Dear friends, we should love each other, because love comes from God. Everyone who loves has become God's child and knows God. Whoever does not love does not know God, because God is love.**
>
> **1 John 4:7–8**

Here is a very important question for you to answer: How can your boyfriend really love you when he does not know God? You see, since he doesn't know God, he doesn't have God's love. Without God's love, he doesn't have the power to love you as God wants him to. Of course, he says he loves you, but according to your letter you can't even get him to go to church. It's painful to admit that your boyfriend doesn't really love you, but it's true, because love is not self-destructive.

Actually, I would expect your non-Christian boyfriend to want to have as much sex with you as he can. Why wouldn't he? He's living for himself. He has no reason to love you God's way or show self-control. He doesn't know God. The fact that you are having ongoing premarital sex with your boyfriend proves that what you have is not real love. In fact, according to Ephesians 5, it is the opposite.

> **Live a life of love. Love other people just as Christ loved us. . . . But there must be no sexual sin among you, or any kind of evil or greed.**
>
> **Ephesians 5:2–3**

Gloria, as you can see in this passage, God commands us to "Live a life of love." In dating, love means choosing to treat the other person with respect and consideration. It means choosing to do what is best for the other person. And it means never intentionally doing anything to hurt the other person, now or in the future. Unfortunately, when we become emotionally involved with someone, we often lose perspective. This is especially true when sex is involved. The emotions caused by premarital sex can seem like love. But as we have seen, premarital sex is not real love. It is really a counterfeit love.

24

Let me ask you an important question. What do you think your boyfriend means when he says, "I love you"? Here's what I believe he's really saying: "I love me, and I like what you give to me!" He knows that sleeping with you is hurting you, but he won't stop. Getting his own needs met is more important to him than the pain he's causing you. That's not love, that's selfishness. Your emotions may be telling you it's love, but the facts say it's not. More important, God's Word says it's not. Though it seems real at the time, Ephesians 5:2–3 makes it very clear that premarital sex and real love are opposites.

There's something else I want you to understand clearly. Unless your boyfriend becomes a Christian and is committed to following God, the chances of your relationship lasting are almost zero. A relationship that is not centered in Christ can only stand so much pressure. It's only a matter of time before fear, guilt, anger, and frustration will cause the relationship to split up. Here's the way I see it: If you express your feelings to your boyfriend, he's eventually going to walk away. And if you don't tell him how you feel, then you are going to become so emotionally upset that you won't be able to go on. Therefore, I am convinced that your relationship with your boyfriend has no real future. Sooner or later it's going to fall apart.

Gloria, there is one more very important thing that you must understand. Your relationship with your boyfriend is doing great damage to your relationship with God. God wants you to turn away from your sin and come back to Him. He loves you so much that He is putting His loving pressure on you right now, and He knows exactly how to do it, too. In the Old Testament,

King David also had a struggle with sexual sin. In Psalm
32, he describes the loving pressure God put on him.

> **When I kept things to myself,**
> **I felt weak deep inside me.**
> **I moaned all day long.**
> **Day and night you punished me.**
> **My strength was gone as in the summer**
> **heat.**
> **Then I confessed my sins to you**
> **and didn't hide my guilt.**
> **I said, "I will confess my sins to the LORD,"**
> **and you forgave my guilt.**
>
> **Psalm 32:3–5**

Judging from your letter, it seems that God is
already "tightening the screws" on your life. You may
be stubborn, but not stubborn enough to withstand
God's strong but loving discipline.

What, then, should you do? I think the answer is
obvious. I think you've known what to do for months
and months. Now it's time for you to go before God and
ask Him to forgive you for your sins against Him. In
order to show Him that you are truly sorry, you must
completely break up with your non-Christian boyfriend.
Jesus said, "Why do you call me 'Lord, Lord' and do not
do what I say?" (Luke 6:46 NIV). The longer you wait to
break it off with your boyfriend, the harder it's going to
be. You must do it now! Gloria, I want you to know that
this will probably be the hardest and most painful thing
you have ever done. I'm hurting with you, but I will
also be thrilled with you because at last you will be
doing the right thing.

26

I think you need to find a Christian counselor as well. This counselor will help you with your emotional addiction to your boyfriend and help you sort through your fears of being rejected and being alone. In order for you to be completely healed from these things, you must come face to face with yourself. In the power of Christ, you must stare down the Gloria who is terrified of being abandoned. You must come to believe that God loves you and will meet your deepest needs. He doesn't want you to be unloved, abandoned, or depressed. He loves you far more than you and I can ever imagine. He has dreams and plans for you that are so wonderful they will blow your mind. However, you must learn to believe Him. You need to let God be God. You must quit trying to be your own god and wait on Him to give you what's best for you at the right time.

Gloria, this is going to be hard, but you can do it. You must do it. The stakes are so high, you must do the right thing. I am convinced you will. Give God a chance to do something great in your life, and you will never be sorry you did.

Your friend,
Dawson

A Letter from Bobby

Dawson,

Since age nine I have been a Christian. I attended your conference last year and was deeply blessed.

Over the past six months, I've fallen out of God's will. Last spring I met a girl who I thought I was in love with. After seventeen years of waiting for the right person, and ignoring the fact that practically all of my friends had had sex, I let myself go with her. After some time it started getting out of hand. She wanted to get pregnant and I was "put on the spot" several times. You would think this decision would be easy for a good strong Christian, and you see, you're right. She had weakened my walk with God to the point I could no longer easily say no. All day long at school I thought of nothing but her. My grades went down and I was put on restrictions. My family hated her because they thought she wasn't the right person for me. Again and again, time after time, people would tell me what a mistake I was making, but I ignored them and put her above all else, even God. A few weeks ago we decided to break up, and I am presently trying to get my life back on track.

Please tell my friends in the audience how premarital sex destroys their lives. It hurts me to see people, even "Christians," who wouldn't think twice about getting laid.

If after this conference we go back to our old lifestyles, nothing has happened. We are here to make a change, but can we make a difference if we aren't different?

Sincerely,
Bobby

Dear Bobby,

I've just finished reading your amazing letter. I have to admit that there aren't that many guys your age who could share both their situation and their feelings as clearly as you have. However, I can assure you that there are many guys, Christian and otherwise, who are in your situation. A lot of times when we talk about the misuse of sex, we talk about girls who get

28

mixed up with the wrong guys. More and more we are seeing guys who are getting hurt by dating the wrong girls. With that in mind, let's have a man-to-man talk about your situation and discover how you got into this mess.

To begin with, it is obvious from your letter that you were dating the wrong woman. Here is a girl who has tremendous emotional and spiritual needs. Quite obviously, she was not surrendering those needs to Jesus Christ. She was openly sexually active, and no doubt, enticing. In the end you gave in to the temptation of going all the way with her.

You know, Bobby, most men do not understand the power of a woman over them, for good or for bad. God made men for women and women for men. A godly couple can provide tremendous love and encouragement for each other. However, when we fail to do what God asks us to do in a relationship, disaster strikes. As you have very painfully learned, this girl was bad news for you. Getting involved with the wrong kind of woman can be a horrible trap for any Christian man. King Solomon, the wisest man in the Bible, put it this way:

> **I found that some women are worse than
>   death
>   and are as dangerous as traps.
> Their love is like a net,
>   and their arms hold men like chains.
> A man who pleases God will be saved from
>   them,
>   but a sinner is caught by them.**
>
> **Ecclesiastes 7:26**

Of course, Bobby, we don't want to just rip on women. The Bible also says that women can be wonderful for men.

**It is hard to find a good wife
because she is worth more than rubies.**

Proverbs 31:10

Therefore, you need to understand that God does have a wonderful woman for you, one who is priceless. But if you fool around with the wrong kind of women, you will pay a very dear price. The next time you come across a woman who isn't living for Jesus and you find yourself attracted to her, get as far away from her as fast as you can. Make Proverbs 5:8 your plan of action.

**Stay away from such a woman.
Don't even go near the door of her house.**

Proverbs 5:8

Not only did you get involved with the wrong woman, but you let your emotions control your life. I am convinced that having sex with this girl stirred up your emotions in a big way. The Bible says,

Above all else, guard your affections. **For they influence everything else in your entire life.**

Proverbs 4:23 TLB

It is obvious that she and your emotions had gotten almost total control of your life. As you said in your letter, "All day long at school I thought of nothing but her. My grades went down and I was put on restrictions."

30

One of the things wrong with our emotions is that we can't always trust them. That's why we must guard our affections. If we're not careful, they can take us in a wrong direction. Once that happens, it's almost always a one-way ticket down the road to heartbreak. The Bible talks about this in Jeremiah.

> **The heart is more deceitful than all else**
> **And is desperately sick;**
> **Who can understand it?**
>
> **Jeremiah 17:9 NASB**

I can tell from your letter that you are beginning to grasp just how badly you fooled yourself over this troubled girl. You allowed your emotions and your actions to get completely out of control. This leads me to the third reason you got into trouble. You refused to listen to the counsel of those around you. You said in your letter, "My family hated her because they thought she wasn't the right person for me. Again and again, time after time, people would tell me what a mistake I was making, but I ignored them and put her above all else, even God." When people who love you are all telling you the same thing, their advice is almost always right. Unfortunately, you had become like the person who said, "My mind is made up, don't confuse me with the facts." You now know how foolish you had become. You refused to listen to wise counsel. The Bible talks about this problem in Proverbs 12.

> **A fool thinks he needs no advice, but a wise**
> **man listens to others.**
>
> **Proverbs 12:15 TLB**

What a mess you were in! I know it's going to take time to get over all of the emotional pain and regrets you have. Still, God was gracious to you. He saved you from getting this girl pregnant like she wanted. He has helped you to see where you have gone wrong. He has forgiven you, and I know that He has a great future for you. I just hope that you will never forget these hard lessons that you have learned.

I certainly agree with you that there are many Christian students who are caught up in the kind of trap you were in. When we get caught in the trap, we are not nearly as effective for God as He intended us to be. In many ways we Christians have become just like the lost world we are trying to reach. You ask a simple question at the very end of your letter. You ask, "We are here to make a change, but can we make a difference if we aren't different?" The answer to your question is simple. The answer is no.

Your friend,
Dawson

2

Broken and Dysfunctional Families

"My Mom is an alchoholic—
she also uses drugs . . . .
Tonight she was so drunk
I had to help her get
undressed."
—Linda

WHEN IT COMES TO THE AMERICAN TEENAGER, I have a favorite saying. I'm sure you've heard it before. "All roads lead to home." To me this line means that the spiritual and emotional health of a student can almost always be traced back to home. To put it another way, the choices we make throughout our lives, for good or for bad, are greatly influenced by what happens in our homes when we are growing up. A recent survey of American Psychological Association members supports this thought. They overwhelmingly believed that the decline of the family unit is the single greatest threat to American mental health.

In my own ministry I have found that nothing gets to students' hearts more quickly than talking about their families. Several years ago we did a prime time TV special called "Making Peace with Dad." The program contained many interviews with students talking about their fathers. We were amazed at the deep emotional pain that came out of nearly every student. There is so much damage and destruction in our homes, even our Christian homes, that it is hard to imagine.

- Roughly 50 percent of all marriages will end in divorce.

- At one time or another nearly half of all students will live in a broken home.
- 12.5 million kids now live in single-parent households.

Behind these statistics are real teenagers with real heartaches— heartaches that, in some cases, never go away. These teens are emotionally damaged; they are spiritually confused, and many have fallen into lifestyles that are horribly self-destructive. I have received many letters from students like these. For this chapter I have chosen a couple that represent different kinds of situations.

First, there is Linda. Poor Linda is the victim of a broken home that is still out of control. She is overwhelmed by her situation and totally clueless about what to do about it. Linda's thoughts and emotions are typical of those of many teenagers in her situation. These students have been burdened with problems that they are way too young to understand or deal with.

Then there is Cheryl. Cheryl lives in a dysfunctional home. Like most students in her situation, she has become furious and disgusted with her parents. But Cheryl's problems go even further than Linda's. Though she started out as a victim, she has begun to act out her anger, adding even more problems to an already-troubled home.

What would your answer be to these letters from Linda and Cheryl? Can they be rescued? Yes, but they need the help of caring students and adults who will patiently lead them to find the wisdom and power available through Jesus Christ. Let's take a look at their problems.

A Letter from Linda

Dear Dawson,

I have been having a lot of family problems. My mom is an alcoholic, she also uses drugs (but not very often). We have had family services over four times. I am fourteen years old and I always have to babysit for my younger brother and three younger sisters. It's not so much as I mind babysitting, but every time I do my mom seems to come home drunk like she did tonight. She was so drunk I had to help her get undressed. I don't know how to help her. I just want to leave (move away) so I won't have to deal with it. I pray for her all the time, but it just doesn't seem to help. Please give me some advice on how to deal with what's going on in my life. I just feel like giving up.

Sincerely,
Linda

Dear Linda,

Thank you for your letter. It is one of the shortest I've ever received. I counted less than 150 words. Yet word for word it has more pain in it than any letter I have ever received. There is no question in my mind that you are a victim of someone else's sin and irresponsibility. You are suffering in ways that no person your age should ever have to suffer. My first reaction was to be angry at what is happening to you. Then I found myself feeling very sad. I am hurting with you and I want to help. But there's no use pretending with you, Linda; you are living in a difficult situation. To you it probably seems impossible. Nonetheless, God is not

38

confused about how to solve your problem. There is a way out for you, and with God's help we are going to find it.

I want you to know that I've read and thought and prayed about your letter. It is obvious that much of your world is out of your control. When you are feeling that helpless it is easy to lose hope. However, I am convinced that there is hope for you. Though it may seem impossible to you, God can bring you through your family problems. He can rescue someone who is young and fragile and in an awful environment. He can make something wonderful of anyone's life who trusts in Him. God has proven He can do this because He did it with His own Son, Jesus Christ. In Isaiah 53 the prophet explained just how weak Christ was when He was growing up and how difficult His circumstances were.

> **He grew up like a small plant before the Lord, like a root growing in a dry land.**
> **Isaiah 53:2a**

The Bible says Jesus grew up like a small plant. You've seen a small plant. It's so fragile that it's easily broken or killed if stepped on. Nonetheless, God was faithful to His son, Jesus. Even though He was fragile growing up, God protected Him. Linda, I know that you're also young and fragile. You're just fourteen and are facing problems that someone much older and more experienced than you would have a difficult time facing. But God will protect and strengthen you just like He did Jesus.

Isaiah also said that Jesus was like a root growing in a dry land. A root growing in a dry land is like a small tree growing in the desert. It gets very little nourishment and is almost sure to die. As a young boy, Jesus faced circumstances in His life that gave Him very little nourishment. He grew up in a time when few people really loved God. He lived under the Roman Empire where some of the top officials in that cruel government wanted to kill Him. His own family misunderstood Him, and the people in His home town tried to kill Him. Yet, with God's help He flourished and became the greatest person who ever lived.

Linda, in a way you are like a root growing in a dry land. Like Jesus, you, too, are facing some very difficult circumstances. But even as young as you are, I want to challenge you. Don't let the hard things you're going through keep you from being all that God wants you to be. Unfortunately, you don't have complete control of your circumstances. Even so, God can make you strong in the middle of them. He can help you grow so that you come out of this awful situation far stronger than you ever dreamed.

Let me tell you one thing that already encourages me about your letter. You seem to be in touch with at least some of your own feelings. That's good. It would be a big mistake for you to pretend that these feelings don't exist. It's far healthier to admit that you have them. Once you've taken the first step of admitting your painful emotions to yourself, then you can take the next step of allowing God to help you deal with them. According to 1 Peter 5:7, that's exactly what He wants you to do.

> **Give all your worries to him, because he cares for you.**
>
> **1 Peter 5:7**

40

You're carrying way too much weight on your shoulders. I know you love your mother, but she has forced you to take on the responsibility of being the mother while she acts like a child. In addition, she has forced you into taking on the care of your brother and sisters. It was never God's plan to burden you, or any fourteen-year-old girl, with the duty of being a mother to four other children. I think these burdens may be causing you to struggle with some really negative emotions. To begin with, I sense that you are horribly embarrassed by your mother's behavior. It must have been humiliating to have to undress your mom because she was too drunk to find her own buttons. It had to make you feel so helpless. If I were you, I would have felt humiliated and helpless, but I also would have been angry!

Linda, I also sense that you are really discouraged because you've had very little help from others. It's bad enough that you've had to suffer the embarrassment of having family services come to the house four times, but you must be really frustrated that they haven't done anything to help you. If anyone has a good reason to feel trapped and totally overwhelmed by circumstances, it's you. No wonder you want to run away. It seems like the only way to deal with your problems.

Linda, I don't totally understand all of the painful and confusing emotions you must be feeling, but God does. In the Old Testament, King David struggled with all kinds of emotional pain. In Psalm 94 he tells about his own experience with feelings of being overwhelmed.

> I said, "I am about to fall," but, LORD, your
> love kept me safe. I was very worried, but you
> comforted me and made me happy.
>
> **Psalm 94:18–19**

King David found that God was there for him no matter how awful he felt. Linda, God has not changed. He loves you every bit as much as he loved King David. He is there for you and will help you. As it did for King David, His love will make you safe. He will comfort you and make you very happy.

Linda, I know that you want more than simply to hear that God loves you or to hear that He will help you. You want some specific answers about how to deal with your terrible situation. That's what I'd want, too. After all, we need to do more than talk about your problems. We need to try and solve them. Let me give you some practical suggestions. The things that I am about to tell you will not be easy for you to do, but I believe that God will give you the courage you need to do them.

First, you must find a Christian adult who will listen to your problems and help you deal with them. Your problems are far too big for you to carry alone. You need someone to help you carry part of this burden. This adult friend will also protect you and help you face your difficult situation one step at a time. I believe that God already has a person like that for you. You need to start right now by asking God to lead you to this person. Then you need to go to the pastor of your church and tell him about your situation. If you're not comfortable with that, go to a youth worker or Sunday school teacher. But you need to find a Christian adult to help you.

Second, you need to get help for your mother. Linda, your mother is a very sick woman, and she needs to be rescued for her own survival. It is going to be very painful for you to reveal your mother's problems by yourself. That's why I am encouraging you to work with your adult friend to tell this story to those who can help her. Your mother is so sick that she needs to be taken out of the home and put in a hospital situation to overcome her alcohol addiction. If she doesn't get help, her problems will only get worse, affecting not only you, but your younger brother and sisters, as well. You must scream loud enough so that the authorities will finally get the picture that your mother is out of control and needs immediate attention.

I can't promise you that things will get better overnight. They may get worse before they get better. But I can assure you that running away is not the answer. It will just lead to more problems. The streets are no place for a fourteen-year-old girl. In addition, your mother's sickness will only get worse and worse, and your brother and sisters will only become bigger victims. I know that you've prayed and that God hasn't seemed to answer. But perhaps He is answering you through this letter. Linda, follow the counsel that I've given you. Trust God to help you through the tough days ahead. Keep believing that your courageous actions will help your mother get well. And finally, have faith that the hard steps you're about to take will be the beginning of a whole new life for you.

One other thing. No matter what you do, don't give up! Don't give up believing God will do great things in your life, and don't give up on yourself. You are far too important and special. God loves you, and He has a bright future for you. You watch and see.

Your friend,
Dawson

A Letter from Cheryl

Dear Dawson,

My name is Cheryl. I've listened to your show a few times and the shows I've listened to really made me think. Anyway, here's my problem.

My parents are divorced. They have been since I was three years old; I'm now fifteen. I live with my stepfather, mother, and half sister. I visit my father, stepmother and stepbrother every other weekend during the school year, six weeks in the summer, and every other year on holidays, also half of school vacations. My father is a Christian, my mother is not, I am. I once asked my mother if I could live with my dad. She said no, and her reaction was the worst thing I've ever lived through in my life thus far. . . . She came close to hitting me. She threw me on my bed. That night I will never forget. . . . That was about six months ago. . . . I'm pretty sure that's when I started to resent her so much. . . . I would still like to live with my dad, or at least change visitation arrangements, possibly shared custody. I am deathly afraid to ask my mom again, and my dad doesn't have the money to take my mom to court again. . . .

I was at my dad's house for the last six weeks of this summer. When I got home it was like I was a different person. It seems I can no longer be happy at home. It's even hard for me to call it home. See, my mom and stepdad both drink and are drunk quite often. They never do anything like hit me or my half sister when they're drunk. I just don't like it. I don't have a problem being a Christian at home, but at my dad's it's really nice to have two great Christian role models. I miss it. One of the worst things about living with my mom is that I feel so much disgust and resentment toward her. Well, I think that's what it is, anyway. I can't really even look at her eye to eye without having to hold back tears. And then there's my step-dad, whom I despise. Well, I guess I don't despise him, but you know, he never says one nice thing to me. That's how my mom is, too. They are both so negative.

Well, the reason I wrote is to get some advice and some scriptures that will help me along and to pray about. My step-mom suggested calling my social worker, but the truth is, I'm very afraid of what will happen. . . . I guess I've never forgiven my mother for all that went on that night, but I don't know how. Thanks for helping.

Cheryl

Dear Cheryl,

I want to thank you for taking the time to pour out your problems to me. I am encouraged that our radio shows have made you think. I am quite certain that, together, we can think through how you can solve your dilemma concerning your parents.

What I am going to share with you may be painful. It may even make you angry. But I hope you'll be open-minded and give this letter a chance to soak into your heart—don't just read it once and blow it off. I want to encourage you to read it several times during the next few weeks. Then I want you to pray about it. As you do these things, remember that God loves you. If you are willing to do His will, I am convinced that He will show you what you need to do.

It is clear to me that you live in a very painful situation over which you don't have much control. You said in your letter that your parents are divorced and have been since you were very young. You also spoke of living with your mother, stepfather, and half sister, and you explained the visiting arrangements with your father, stepmother, and stepbrother. Then you stated that you and your father are Christians while your mother is not.

First of all, I want you to understand clearly that it's not your fault that your parents are divorced. At the time it happened you were only a baby. It is also obvious that you have no control over which set of parents you live with. That decision has been made for you. Third, no one can blame you that your "mom and stepdad both drink and are drunk quite often." That's a choice that they have made on their own. And fourth, you're just now fifteen. That means that until you turn eighteen there is very little you can do to change your circumstances.

However, there is something that you can change. You can change yourself. Cheryl, you can't control your situation, but you can change your attitudes toward your situation. I know it won't be easy, but it is something that, with God's help, you can learn to do. That's what I want to talk to you about in this letter.

It is obvious to me that you would rather live with your real dad and stepmother. You made your reasons for this very clear when you said you were a different person when you returned to your mother's house after being at your father's. Cheryl, I think you're convinced that moving in with your father and stepmother will solve all of your problems and take away all of your pain. However, I don't think that's true. Portions of your letter are filled with anger and resentment toward your mom and stepfather—anger and resentment that you've never dealt with. Until you begin to overcome these feelings you won't be emotionally and spiritually ready to leave, even if your mother changes her mind and lets you go.

You also talked about how you felt when your mom got mad at you for asking to live with your dad and how she threw you on your bed. You said, "I'm pretty sure that's when I started to resent her so much. I guess I've never forgiven my mother for all that went on that night, but I don't know how." Cheryl, I want you to know that I really admire your honesty. It can be very difficult to talk about how much someone has hurt you and how angry that has made you. But now I want you to be honest again. I want you to take a look at the words and phrases you used to describe your relationship with your mom and stepfather: disgust, resentment, despise, they are both so negative, resent her, I've never forgiven her. These are hard and bitter words. They are clear evidence of the painfully negative emotions that are locked inside you. Yes, I'm sure that moving to your dad's house would help you feel better about some things, but I don't think it would solve what I think is your major problem: You simply haven't forgiven your mom and stepfather for all that they have done to you.

Cheryl, your anger and resentment will follow you into adulthood. These emotions will eat away at you, and eventually they will hurt you far more than you can imagine. In fact, in Ephesians, the Bible implies that when we become bitter and resentful toward our parents it may hurt us more than it hurts them.

"Honor your father and mother"—which is the first commandment with a promise—"that it may go well with you and that you may enjoy long life on the earth."

Ephesians 6:2 NIV

God promises us that if we honor our parents, that is, if we obey them and respect them, it is very likely that we will live a long, enjoyable life. But, Cheryl, the opposite is also true. If we refuse to honor our parents, it is almost certain that our lives will be much shorter and sadder. This is true because resentment toward our parents eats us up on the inside. It creates what psychologists call negative stress. Much of the pain you are feeling right now is negative stress created by not honoring your parents. This negative stress can lead to all kinds of health problems, such as depression, ulcers, heart trouble, and even cancer. So you see, when you refuse to work at healing a broken relationship, you really are letting yourself in for misery God never intended for you.

I read a book several years ago about how a man should treat his wife. The title was, *Do Yourself a Favor, Love Your Wife.* For you, the title of the book could just as easily be, *Do Yourself a Favor, Honor Your Parents.* I

48

hope you're starting to understand that God never intended for you to be weighed down with anger and resentment toward your mom and stepfather. Emotionally and physically it's much too heavy a burden for you to carry. In fact, not only will a broken relationship hurt you, but it will hurt others as well. The Bible talks about this in Hebrews.

> **Be careful that no one fails to receive God's grace and begins to cause trouble among you. A person like that can ruin many of you.**
>
> **Hebrews 12:15**

Do you want to be a person like this? One who not only ruins herself, but has the potential to ruin others? It is a real possibility. For example, you will come in contact with people daily who remind you of your mother or stepfather. It could be a teacher at school, or a friend, or even your future husband. Because of this reminder, being around them will stir up your bitter memories and fuel your anger all the more. This anger only creates barriers between yourself and others. Sometimes it can even cause people to become angry back at you. All you're doing is creating a cycle of anger and destruction that will hurt many innocent people.

Cheryl, the fact of the matter is, you must, in the power of Christ, forgive your mother and stepfather. Moreover, you must learn to honor them. What I am asking you to do is difficult, but in Christ's power it is not impossible. I know this is true because God commands that we forgive others who have wronged us.

> Bear with each other and forgive whatever
> grievances you may have against one another.
> Forgive as the Lord forgave you.
>
> **Colossians 3:13** NIV

What does it mean to forgive others? Basically, it means this: I forgive others when I give up my right to get even with them for the pain they have caused me. To put it another way, I am going to let go of my negative emotions toward those who have hurt me in the past so that those emotions will not affect my response toward them in the present.

In a real sense, you have every reason to be resentful and bitter. After all, your parents divorced when you were just a baby. Your mother physically abused you. Your mom and stepfather have a drinking problem, and they never seem to have anything good to say about you. But, Cheryl, you need to understand that God knows how much your parents have hurt you. He is deeply grieved that all this has happened to you. Yet He says, "Forgive as the Lord forgave you."

Cheryl, in spite of what has happened to you, God wants you to forgive your parents just as He forgave you. Let me explain this so that you clearly understand what I am saying. God had every right to punish us in eternal hell for all of the horrible things we have done against Him. Yet He chose to forgive us by allowing His Son, Jesus Christ, to die on the cross and take the punishment for our sins. Once we have accepted Christ's death on our behalf, God refuses even to think about our sins. Instead, He concentrates on ways to show His love and forgiveness to us. Because of God's love at the

50

cross, He refuses to think about getting even with us or paying us back. Instead, He is devoted to loving us and preparing a home in heaven for us for all of eternity. God let go of all His anger and negative emotions toward us through His gift in Christ, which now allows God to completely forgive us.

In much the same way that God has forgiven us, He wants us to forgive others. Forgiving your parents does not mean that you forget what they did to you—you might never forget what your parents did to you. What forgiving your parents does mean is that now you refuse to get even with them. Instead, you are free to think of ways you can love them as if they had never hurt you.

Colossians 3:13 tells us another important ingredient in forgiveness—"Bear with each other." Bearing with each other means more than forgiving people for what has happened in the past. It means that even when their weaknesses and failures cause you new pain, you choose to refuse to get angry and bitter again. Cheryl, it is important for you to realize that your parents won't change overnight. They will hurt you again. Therefore, you must be committed to toughing it out with them. Remember, God bears with your weaknesses every day, and He wants you to do the same with your troubled parents.

I realize that forgiving your parents will be one of the most difficult things you have ever done. But you must do it, and in God's power you *can* do it. Someday God may want you to move in with your father and stepmother. But at least for the time being, God wants you to learn the lesson of forgiveness right where you are.

Cheryl, I want to give you several practical suggestions that may help your situation. Thus far we have talked about how God wants you to forgive your parents and change your whole attitude toward them. However, God is not asking you to stay in a home where there is physical and deep emotional abuse. Therefore, it is absolutely critical that you find a counselor who will help you—possibly your youth worker, a teacher, or even a social worker. The important thing is that it's someone you trust and who knows Christ.

This counselor can help you work through several things. A good counselor will help you find ways to express your feelings. When you express your feelings to a counselor, they do not stay bottled up until they explode. Getting your feelings out to someone who cares for you and will listen is the beginning of the healing process.

A good counselor will help you and your parents communicate with each other. This will help both sides work out the pain and misunderstanding. Because the counselor is a neutral third party, he or she can do a better job of sorting out the negative emotions in a broken relationship.

Finally, a counselor will be able to tell whether or not you are being so abused in your home that you must leave. However, if that time should come, it does not change your responsibility to forgive your parents and bear with them.

Cheryl, I hope this letter has helped you. I am aware that the things you need to do to heal the relationship with your parents will be very difficult. But in the end, it will be worth every bit of the struggle.

52

Remember, God deeply loves you, and He wants you to succeed. In fact, He has written a very special promise in the Book of Philippians that applies perfectly to you.

> **I can do all things through Christ, because he gives me strength.**
>
> **Philippians 4:13**

I know you can do it!

Your friend,
Dawson

3

Suicide

"Life is stupid. I hate myself for feeling like this because something says it's a sin. I screwed up again, and I'm so sick of stupid me screwing up. I feel like I live a lie."

—*Julie*

THERE IS HARDLY ANYTHING MORE TROUBLING TO ME than to view the body of a teenager in a coffin. It just doesn't seem right. Teenagers are so alive and full of hope and idealism. They have so much ahead of them. But what really disturbs me is viewing the body of a student who has chosen to kill himself. What a tragedy. How does one so young become so full of despair and rage?

The sad truth is that teenagers are thinking about suicide, attempting suicide, and succeeding at suicide like never before. In fact, they have been so "successful" that suicide now kills more fifteen- to nineteen-year-olds than any cause other than accidents. A recent Gallup poll reports:

- One third of U.S. teenagers say they have thought about suicide.
- 15 percent have come up with some kind of plan.
- 6 percent have actually attempted suicide.

Let's look at these statistics and the way they might affect your neighborhood. If we suppose that your high school has a student body of about 1,500 students, then our Gallup poll would look like this:

- 500 students would have thought about suicide.
- 225 students would have come up with some kind of plan to kill themselves.
- 90 students would have actually attempted suicide.

Obviously, anyone who actually attempts suicide has become extremely confused and desperate. I believe students attempting suicide are sending one of two messages to those around them. The first message is, "I want someone to listen to me and understand my pain." These students don't really want to die, but they are desperate for attention and help. Unfortunately, these students run the risk of accidentally killing themselves. They also are telling us that they are one step closer to a successful attempt.

The second and the more deadly message sent by students who attempt suicide is, "I would rather face the unknown of death than have to deal with the awful reality of life." Most of these students don't want to die. They're just afraid to go on living.

I have received many letters from suicidal students, but the one I want to share is from a girl named Julie. Her letter is typical of the way most suicidal students think. I know that Julie, and those like her, can be rescued from their despair. If God's Word is anything, it is truth for the confused, hope for the hopeless, and love for the unloved. I hope my answer to Julie's troubled letter will give you some insight on how to deal with a suicidal student.

A Letter from Julie

Dawson,

Hi—My name is Julie and I'm sixteen. I want to die. Things are so confusing and stupid. This world would be a better place if I wasn't here to worry about. I was listening to your program "Dawson McAllister . . . Live" just now and you were talking about suicide. I haven't got the guts to call the Hope Line, so I'm writing instead. The hardest thing is that you say that Jesus is a way out and you pray to Him. I used to be a Christian, but now I don't know if I am anymore. Why would God love me? . . .

People have lectured to me about turning this whole situation over to God, but it's not that simple. God was the only thing that kept me hanging on as long as I could, and when He left the world crashed. It's strange that I'm even here today because I hadn't planned to be—that was five months ago when my youth director saved my life. Things were shook up at first, but now everything is pretty much back to normal in everyone else's life. I guess it doesn't matter that I still hurt. Mom and Dad just get upset and embarrassed that their "perfect" daughter could be having problems. It seems like they think ignoring suicide will make it go away. Well, it's still in my mind and I'm so frustrated that I want to do it again. If life and death is supposed to be decided by God, but there is no God, then maybe I'll have to decide for myself. I'm so sick of trying to hang on. Where is God? I want to get high or trip out on acid because at least then maybe I would have fun. Life is stupid. I hate myself for feeling like this because something says it's a sin. I screwed up again and I'm so sick of stupid me screwing up. I feel like I live a lie.

58

I started a new school last fall. It's a smaller, Christian school in place of my former large public school. It is very strict. They can form and change the outside with dress codes and rules, but they can't change what's going on inside. It tears me apart. If I screw up or don't meet the model Christian standards I'll be kicked out. I don't know if I want to become a Christian if Christians aren't allowed to make mistakes. How could God love me anyway? . . . I really mess things up and I don't know where I went wrong, so I can't fix them anymore. I don't think that it's worth trying because that's what I have been doing for over a year. Who could forgive and love me anyway? There is no such thing as perfect love. Everyone keeps their love to themselves to be sure that they will have enough. I just want a hug that asks for no perfection in return. I know that that is not possible, so I might as well quit wasting my time looking.

I feel guilty for even thinking like this and writing it to you. I'm sure that God hates it, too. I'm afraid of living and afraid of dying, and I sit balanced between the two. This is stupid and here I am in the middle of it. I don't understand why, how, or what. I'm "the problem" as my dad would say, so I guess that I better fix it. I just wish I had a clue as to why, how or what to do. I live a worthless life and I hate it. Everyone does. Where is God? Help! I can't handle it anymore, and I'm sick of hanging on to nothing. I want to die or get away or get high.

Any insights? Thanks for listening!
Julie

Dear Julie,

Thank you for your letter. I have thought long and hard about your situation. I want you to know that I care about you, and that is why I am going to tell you the truth, even if the truth hurts. I can tell by several things that you said in your letter that you are truly confused. For example, you said, "I want to die. Things are so confusing and stupid. . . . I really mess things up and I don't know where I went wrong, so I can't fix them anymore. I don't think that it's worth trying because that's what I have been doing for over a year. . . . This is stupid and here I am in the middle of it. I don't understand why, how, or what."

Julie, from your point of view, your whole world seems to be coming apart. I'm sure you feel like no one is even listening to you, let alone understanding your situation. You're feeling very alone, and you're trying to make sense out of your life all by yourself. That makes it almost impossible to get any kind of perspective on your situation. There is not a person alive who hasn't fallen into this trap at some time. God never intended for us to try and make sense of life's problems all by ourselves. In fact, in Proverbs 3 He tells us exactly the opposite.

> **Trust the Lord with all your heart, and don't depend on your own understanding. Remember the Lord in all you do, and he will give you success.**
>
> **Proverbs 3:5–6**

As you can see from this Scripture passage, God tells us not to depend on our own understanding. In other words, don't try to make sense of life by yourself. God knows that when our thoughts and emotions become confused we almost always distort reality. We distort what has happened to us in the past, what is happening to us in the present, and what is likely to happen to us in the future. That's why we need to trust God to help us. He sees and understands all of life—past, present and future—and has the answers to all of our problems.

Let's take a look at some of the things that are troubling you. First of all, you are confused about God's love. It seems that you have come to the mistaken conclusion that God does not love you. In fact, it sounds like you believe that you are unlovable. You said, "I used to be a Christian, but now I don't know if I am anymore. Why would God love me?" Then you ask, "Who could forgive and love me anyway? There is no such thing as perfect love."

Julie, I am convinced that God loves you more than you will ever know. The problem is we often refuse to accept His love. Your question, "Why would God love me?" indicates that this is what you have done. Yet, it is an excellent question that deserves an answer. This may not be easy to comprehend, but God loves you *just because.* He has simply chosen to love you, and He refuses to ever stop loving you, no matter what. In Jeremiah, God says,

> **I love you people with a love that will last forever. That is why I have continued showing you kindness.**
> **Jeremiah 31:3**

There is not a person on this earth who deserves God's love—not you, not me, not your youth director. No one *deserves* God's love. Nonetheless, it showers down on us every moment of our existence. You didn't earn God's love because no one can earn God's love. You can't unearn it either. No matter what you do or fail to do, you can't stop God's love from surrounding you every minute of every day. For you to try and separate God's love from you is like someone sitting in a rowboat trying to drain the ocean with an eyedropper in the midst of a torrential rain storm. It's just not going to happen.

You also asked, "Who could forgive and love me, anyway?" And you state, "There is no such thing as perfect love." God has already provided an awesome answer to you.

> **Yes, I am sure that neither death, nor life, nor angels, nor ruling spirits, nothing now, nothing in the future, no powers, nothing above us, nothing below us, nor anything else in the whole world will ever be able to separate us from the love of God that is in Christ Jesus our Lord.**
>
> **Romans 8:38–39**

Your belief that God does not love you is simply not true. God does love you. He proved it by dying on the cross for you so that you could be forgiven and live at peace with Him forever. I know you don't feel that God loves you. Nevertheless, He does love you, and you need to start thanking Him for that love.

You have also convinced yourself that God has abandoned you. In your letter you said, "God was the only thing that kept me hanging on as long as I could, and when He left, the world crashed. It's strange that I'm even here today because I hadn't planned to be— that was five months ago when my youth director saved my life." I know that you may feel that God has left you, but I promise you that He hasn't. God loves you and is completely committed to you. Think of someone you truly love, someone that you love more than anyone else. Would you leave that person? Would you just abandon him or her? Probably not! God's love is so great that He loves you billions of times more than you or I could ever love anyone! So why would He leave you? God has promised to stay with us and to love us no matter what. And He has put that promise in writing.

> **God said, "I will never leave you; I will never forget you."**
>
> **Hebrews 13:5b**

Julie, God says that He will never leave you, and He never will. NEVER!

There is another area where I think your untrue beliefs are causing you big problems. It seems to me that you are both frustrated and tired. You are frustrated because no matter how hard you try to do better in your life you seem to fail. You are tired because you have tried to do better for a long time and yet continue to fail. Let's face it, you've spent most of your life trying to perform. You said it yourself in you letter: "I screwed up again, and I'm so sick of stupid me screwing up. . . . How could God love me?" You have been caught in a trap that many Christians fall into. This trap causes us to think that we have to perform up to the expectations of others in order for them to love and accept us. Trying to perform for others will always lead us into frustration and exhaustion. It's like being on a treadmill and never being able to get off. You try and try to perform to other people's standards, but sooner or later you can't keep up.

God does not want you on the treadmill of performance. He wants you to know that He accepts and loves you just the way you are. His love for you is not based on your performance. God looks at you through the life, death, and resurrection of His Son, Jesus Christ. The Bible talks about this in Romans.

> **Since we have been made right with God by our faith, we have peace with God. This happened through our Lord Jesus Christ.**
>
> **Romans 5:1**

The Bible says that when we trust Christ He justifies us. In other words, when God looks at you and me, He declares us as pure and holy as His Son, Jesus Christ. The purity of Jesus Christ is called His righteousness. Since God has fully forgiven us for our sins and given us the inexhaustible righteousness of Christ forever, He will always be completely pleased with who we are—*even if we fail.* If you become the most successful person in history, you could not increase your worth to God. If you fail miserably for the rest of your life you cannot decrease your worth to God. He has completely forgiven you for all your sins—past, present, and future. In fact, when God looks at you, He sees the righteousness of Christ. It is the most valuable item in the entire universe and it belongs to you. You need to understand once and for all that you are not performing for God. That means that you don't have to "perform" for anyone else, either. God loves you just the way you are.

64

Julie, it is also very clear that you're trying to solve your problems by using some very destructive solutions. You said in your letter, "I'm so sick of trying to hang on. Where is God? I want to get high or trip out on acid, because at least then maybe I would have fun." Turning to illegal drugs has never solved anyone's problems. In fact, doing drugs will only make you more confused and push you closer and closer to the brink of suicide. In your letter you said, "I'm afraid of living and afraid of dying, and I sit balanced between the two." Your pain has lead you to so many wrong beliefs that suicide appears to be a way to escape. But that's not true. You need to understand clearly what an awful choice suicide really is.

To begin with, God sees suicide as an act of murder. He clearly states this in Ezekiel.

> **Every living thing belongs to me. The life of**
> **the parent is mine, and the life of the child is mine.**
> **The person who sins is the one who will die.**
>
> **Ezekiel 18:4**

The right to begin life and end life is in God's hands. He alone is wise enough to know when life should begin and end. When we kill ourselves we make the horrible mistake of playing God. This not only grieves Him, but leads to the final disastrous act of suicide. When a person commits suicide he becomes the murderer, the victim, the judge, the jury, and the executioner of his crime. God never intended us to take on all of those roles. While suicide alone will not keep us from heaven or God's love, it is a terrible violation of who God is and of His plan for our life.

Julie, before you decide to kill yourself you also need to see that suicide is an unglamorous act of selfishness. Sometimes, in our depression, we can fantasize that suicide is a courageous event. We view it as making a brave choice to leave our painful life behind. Suicide looks like a glamorous way to slip away to a restful eternity and make a statement to those we feel have hurt us. But I have a question for you, Julie. If you kill yourself, who's going to clean up the mess? What about the person who finds your body? How are they going to feel? And what do you think your body is going to look like when it's cold and dead and lifeless? Killing yourself is never just a solo act. It will cause lifelong hurt and pain to many, many people. The Bible says,

We do not live or die for ourselves.

Romans 14:7

Did you know that almost everything we do has some affect on others? For example, if you kill yourself how will that affect what would have been your future husband and children? And what about the pain and the agony that will come upon your parents, family, and friends? Some of these people will never get over the devastation that your suicide would cause. So you see, suicide is an incredibly selfish act.

Finally, in the midst of your depression, suicide may seem like an easy way to escape your problems. However, in reality it's a tragic excuse to avoid facing them. I know that right now your problems seem insurmountable. But please believe me, they aren't! You can take responsibility for your own emotions and actions.

66

In fact, you must! I care about you and I want you to get well. Now is the time to start. You need to get up and get into counseling. You need to promise me, your counselor, and your friends that you'll stop thinking about suicide and start concentrating on getting well. And, most important of all, you need to turn to God. He loves you and wants to give you a full, happy, wonderful life. Come on, Julie, your life is much too precious to throw away. Don't kill yourself. Choose Life!

Your friend,
Dawson

4

Drug and Alcohol Abuse

"I'm so scared. I'm tired of all the hangovers and coming down. I'm tired of running from everything."
—*Traci*

THE FACT THAT STUDENTS ABUSE DRUGS AND ALCOHOL IS OLD NEWS. Everybody knows that many teenagers are users and abusers. But while you and I have gotten used to this fact, the problem has neither gone away nor gotten smaller.

According to a *USA Today* survey, drug use among twelfth graders is at a sixteen-year low. This is good news, but don't get too excited. About half of all high school students still admit to having tried illicit drugs such as marijuana, cocaine, or LSD. Cocaine use was 13 percent in 1978 and is still 12 percent today. And LSD use, 10 percent in 1978, has only dropped slightly to 8 percent today. There is one bright spot. The number of students who use marijuana or heroin has taken a significant drop.

Unfortunately, illegal drugs such as marijuana, cocaine, crack, and LSD account for some, but not all, of the drug use problem. In fact, if you ask students at your high school which drug causes the most problems among teenagers, they will probably tell you it is alcohol. In a survey of student leaders, almost half identified alcohol as their schools' number one problem. This is not surprising. Of all the drugs, alcohol is certainly the easiest for teenagers to get. TV advertising has also influenced students to drink. By the time the average student reaches eighteen, he or she will have seen over 100,000 beer commercials. Only now are we beginning to see the true impact the alcohol industry has made on teenagers.

- 93 percent of America's high school students have used alcohol at some point.
- Teens and adults polled in a 1990 Gallup poll ranked alcohol as the number-one threat to teens.
- Binge drinking is a serious problem. 70 percent of all teenagers who drink frequently (three or more times a week) say they always drink four or more beers each time.
- Government surveys show almost 8 million teenagers drink weekly, and 4.5 million are alcoholics.
- The average age for kids entering treatment centers for alcohol problems is thirteen to fourteen. Just two years ago, it was sixteen or seventeen.

When asked why they drink, half of all teenagers surveyed responded by saying that they drink when they are upset. That's frightening, because I believe that right now, students are more angry, more upset, and more disoriented by their world than teenagers at any time in the twentieth century. And here's another frightening fact: Because of their physical immaturity, it takes an adolescent only one year to reach the advanced stages of alcoholism found in an adult who has been drinking heavily for twenty years.

Of course, most students don't abuse drugs and alcohol just for the fun of it. Usually they are trying to numb the emotional pain in their lives. Unfortunately, it seldom takes long before their substance abuse becomes so destructive that their other problems are overshadowed. This is certainly true in our first letter. Traci was struggling with many problems. She had experienced much rejection in her life. To cover the pain, she began to drink and do drugs. As the pain became more than she could handle, so did her abuse. Soon, the problems created by drugs and alcohol were far greater than just the pain of rejection. Then there's Ray's poem, in which he recounts his friends' self-destructive use of drugs. It's an insightful look into the vicious cycle of drug use, communicated by a student who has felt the heartache of far too much tragedy in his young life.

Nevertheless, there are answers to the problems of drug and alcohol abuse. God, in His Word, goes deeper than these problems, which are really only symptoms. He gets to the heart of the matter. I hope that the letter and poem in this chapter will give you insights and answers that you can apply to your life or the lives of others who may be drug abusers.

A Letter from Traci

Dawson,

I've got an alcohol and drug problem. It's not something little, either. I've got a major problem and I need some help.

. . . . I've been involved with alcohol and drugs now for about six years. I started to experiment back in seventh grade and used on and off through eighth grade. When I was in ninth grade I got more involved and the usage increased. It continued this way through my sophomore year.

My junior year and senior year were mostly filled with hangovers and coming down off drugs. I was getting into more trouble at school but they never thought it was alcohol or drugs, they assumed it was due to all the family problems. I just graduated in May, and since then I have basically been drinking or using constantly. . . .

I'm seriously thinking about joining AA and going for treatment. I don't know what to do, Dawson, I'm so scared. I'm tired of all the hangovers and coming down, I'm tired of running from everything. Last week I lost my job. It was partly due to my drinking and using, at least that's what led up to it. I was the cashier at a cafeteria in town and was responsible for money in the register. I've been running short financially and would dip into the register for what-ever I needed at the time. Last Monday, I got caught and was suspended. . . .

During the last ten months a number of my friends have died. Last October Johnny committed suicide. I had grown up with him all my life, he only lived five houses away from me. We had gone to homecoming together our sophomore year, and now he's gone. The beginning of April, Justin was killed in a motorcycle accident. The middle of July, Kristy was killed in a drunk driving accident. Three weeks later Ron was killed in a motorcycle accident. Two weeks after Ron died, Brian was found dead. The doctors have no idea why he died. That's five friends I've lost in ten months, half of which can be contributed to drugs or alcohol.

Family problems have been all I've known most of the last six or seven years. . . . Most of my senior year I lived with friends on and off because I just couldn't handle that type of an environment anymore. In June I moved out, I had enough of it. Two friends and I got an apartment in town, and we have been struggling like crazy ever since. Please show me there really is some hope. You say you care about teenagers. So many people have told me they care and then turned their backs. Please don't turn yours on me today. I can't take any more rejection or it's all over. Please help me.

Traci

Dear Traci,

Thank you for your letter. After reading it, I am deeply concerned about your drug and alcohol abuse. You were very honest and direct with me about your problems. That's a good sign. I also want to be as honest and direct with you as you were with me. I want you to know that I'm not pulling any punches. Your problems are very serious. They are not so serious, however, that God cannot solve them. I know that you have been deeply hurt by others, yet I think that you have hurt yourself far more than anyone has hurt you. Because of your trauma, I will try to be just as kind and caring as I can be. So, Traci, please allow me to give you some counsel that is from the Bible and is backed up by my own experience. I believe this counsel will help you to break away from your serious addiction. In addition, it may also save you from future consequences that are worse than those that you are now experiencing.

First, it is obvious to me that you have a serious addiction. You have fallen into a classic trap that Satan has used to enslave many people. Your letter shows how

74

your drug and alcohol abuse have sent you slipping steadily downhill into bondage. You said you've been involved with alcohol and drugs now for about six years, starting to experiment as early as seventh grade, and that your use progressed, until your "junior year and senior year were mostly filled with hangovers and coming down off drugs." When you began experimenting with drugs in the seventh grade, you were already beginning to fall into Satan's trap. It is my guess that deep inside you were beginning to look for some kind of relief from the rejection you were feeling in your home. However, on the surface, experimenting with drugs and alcohol was exciting. In seventh and eighth grades, getting high was a thrill because it made you feel really alive. You were also experiencing a thrill of another kind. It's called the thrill of sin. The thrill of sin is doing something that down deep inside you know you really should not do. The Bible talks about this in the Book of Proverbs.

> **Stolen water is sweeter, and food eaten in secret tastes better.**
>
> **Proverbs 9:17**

Unfortunately, Traci, what you didn't understand in the seventh and eighth grades is that Satan was playing a deadly trick on you. He patiently allowed you the thrill that experimenting with sin can bring. He knew you were young, hurting, and easily deceived. I imagine that you actually began to believe that drugs were helping you. Solomon, the wisest man in the Bible, spoke of this kind of deception in Proverbs.

> **Some people think they are doing what's right, but in the end it leads to death.**
>
> **Proverbs 14:12**

Those first two years of experimenting with drugs were big on thrills and small on consequences. But by the time you were in the ninth grade you were into an even more deadly trap. You were caught in the law of diminishing returns. The law of diminishing returns says that it always takes more of what you are doing to maintain your original thrill, whether it's drugs, sex, stealing, or whatever. The law of diminishing returns is a vicious merry-go-round that is almost impossible to get off of. Your letter indicated that this is what happened to you: "When I was in ninth grade I got more involved, and the usage increased. It continued this way through my sophomore year."

So you went from experimenting in the seventh and eighth grades to craving in the ninth and tenth grades. The law of diminishing returns had you firmly in its grip. But you had not yet hit bottom. You had two more years of incredible drug and alcohol abuse ahead of you. Your letter described those years as "mostly filled with hangovers and coming down off drugs." You go on to say that, since you graduated in May, you have, "basically been drinking or using constantly." Traci, reading these words hurts me because it tells me that during these years you were living in an unreal world of addiction. The real you was almost gone, replaced by lies, denial, and confusion. You had become a slave to drugs, and they had become your god. The Bible talks about this sad condition in Isaiah.

> He doesn't know what he is doing; his con-
> fused mind leads him the wrong way. He cannot
> save himself or say, "This statue I am holding is a
> false God."
>
> **Isaiah 44:20**

What started in the seventh grade as big thrills and small consequences has now taken a tragic turn. After six years of looking for higher highs and greater thrills, you have finally discovered the cruel truth: Beating the law of diminishing returns is impossible. Nothing proves this more clearly than your own words: "I don't know what to do, Dawson, I'm so scared. I'm tired of all the hang-overs and coming down, I'm tired of running from everything." Then you lost your job as cashier, partly because of your drinking and using, "at least that's what lead up to it. . . . I've been running short financially and would dip into the register for whatever I needed at the time. Last Monday, I got caught and was suspended."

Traci, what a tragedy. You are now facing the horrible consequences of sin. The sin of drug and alcohol abuse has led you far away from the beauty and purity that God has always planned for you. Now you're self-destructive. And to be painfully honest, you're only a shell of what God intended you to be. Slowly but surely you are dying. The Bible talks about this kind of tragic decline in James 1.

> But people are tempted when their own evil
> desire leads them away and traps them. This de-
> sire leads to sin, and then the sin grows and
> brings death.
>
> **James 1:14–15**

To make matters even worse, God has confronted you with the ultimate consequences of drug and alcohol abuse: physical death. According to your letter, your friends are dying on you right and left; "During the last ten months a number of my friends have died. . . . Johnny . . . Justin . . . Kristy . . . Ron . . . Brian. . . . That's five friends I've lost in ten months, half of which can be contributed to drugs or alcohol." It is an awful thing when close friends die. Incredibly you've seen it five times in the last ten months. You're not only grieving the loss of your friends, but you've realized that you could very well be the next to die. But Traci, you're not ready to die! In fact, I really believe you have hit bottom and now very much want to live.

I know that so far most of what I've shared with you must seem very depressing. Yet, I want you to know that two things in your letter have made me very hopeful. First, you said, "I've got an alcohol and drug problem. It's not something little, either. I've got a major problem and I need some help." Later in your letter you said, "Please show me there really is some hope." I want you to know that you can get help. There is hope. You can escape from the horrible grip of your addiction. You can get free from the destruction of drugs and alcohol, but it won't be easy, and there is a price to be paid. In fact, you're going to need more courage than you ever thought possible. And you'll need to trust God to give you that courage. I believe in you, Traci, and I think that you're ready to get started down the road to recovery. So let's do it!

To begin with, you must admit to God that your life is absolutely out of control. You must admit to Him that what you are doing will kill you unless you stop now.

Next, you must reach out for help. You can't overcome this problem by yourself. Drugs have held you prisoner for far too long for you to simply walk away. You said in your letter that you are seriously thinking about treatment. Do it. Go for treatment. Go into a detox center and get all of that poison out of your body. That will be a great start, but you must understand that the poison in your body is only part of the problem.

You need to admit that you have an even more serious poison in your soul. You have tried to use drugs and alcohol as a means of coping with your problems. Unfortunately, that's like drinking "Drain-O" to fix a stomach ache. It doesn't fix anything, and it's guaranteed to make your problems much worse. Getting the emotional poison out of your soul is going to take long-term counseling. You need to discover what it was that triggered your drug use in the first place. However, I think you already have some clues, because you hinted at them in your letter. Here's what you said: "Family problems have been all I've known most of the last six or seven years. . . . Most of my senior year I lived with friends on and off because I just couldn't handle that type of an environment anymore. In June I moved out, I had enough of it. Two friends and I got an apartment in town, and we have been struggling like crazy ever since. Please show me there really is some hope. You say you care about teenagers. So many people have told me they care and then turned their backs. Please don't turn yours on me today. I can't take any more rejection or it's all over. Please help me."

It seems to me that your biggest problem is not drugs and alcohol. You biggest problem is your belief that you have been rejected. And you made that problem worse by thinking that drugs and alcohol could numb the awful pain of that rejection. Obviously, they couldn't. Therefore, you now need to turn to Christian counseling and Christian friends to help you deal with your deep sense of loss and rejection.

Finally, it's time for you to start trusting God. The only way you can have lasting change is with His help. When Christ died on the cross for you He saw and felt your deep sense of rejection. He understood how horrible your sin of addiction really was. And, knowing that, He took all of that pain and sin on Himself so that you could be set free. Put your trust into this Christ. Believe in His great love for you and in His great power to heal you. When you do, He will not only help you throw off your addiction, but He will begin to change you into someone whole and truly beautiful.

Traci, this is not going to be easy. Turning yourself in for detox is hard. Long-term intense counseling is hard. Making yourself accountable to people who will help you stay off drugs is hard. Yes, it's hard, but you're worth it! In your letter you begged for me not to reject you, and I won't. But even if I should ever fail you, I want you to know that God won't. You are His precious little girl, and He loves you. He wants to help you through this difficult time in your life. In fact, in Isaiah 55 God gave a very beautiful invitation that He wants you to accept right now. For you, it's an invitation to trust Him instead of drugs and alcohol. Do it, Traci, because in Christ, you have a truly wonderful life ahead of you.

The LORD says, "All you who are thirsty, come and drink. Those of you who do not have money,

come, buy and eat! Come buy wine and milk without money and without cost. Why spend your
money on something that is not real food? Why
work for something that doesn't really satisfy you?
Listen closely to me, and you will eat what is good;
your soul will enjoy the rich food that satisfies.
Come to me and listen; listen to me so you may
live.

Isaiah 55:1–3a

I'll be praying for you.

Your friend,
Dawson

A Poem from Ray

A Silver Platter for You

Jenny had problems, her parents abused her.
    They told her she was trash and nothing but a
    loser.
Mike's parents divorced, and he didn't know who
    to pick.
    The things he had to listen to made him
    confused and sick.
Ashley's parents died, and she just didn't know
    what to do.
    She was always very sad and extremely blue.
Jeff had no parents and lived on the street.
    Having no parents or home, he really felt the
    heat.
Jenny, Jeff, Mike, and Ashley were really given a
    bad deal.

They were forced to handle some situations
which were very unreal.

These kind of problems make you feel lost,
depressed, and unwanted.
It's as though the devil is making sure you are
constantly taunted.

Let me make it clear—these were once wonderful
people with wonderful minds,
Who were good at activities of all kinds.

Having no one to talk to or someone who
understands,
They all turned to something that wasn't in
their plans.

It was drugs, their only way out.
Drugs made them feel better without a doubt.

Can't you understand the actions they have
chosen?!!
Their lives miserable and wrecked, full of
mental erosion.

Some of the things they've had to endure,
A million men couldn't handle, and that's for
sure.

So they started a new life of drug use,
That shut away all their horrible abuse.

Though it seemed that when they were on a trip
their problems were gone,
They would come back down and still feel as if
they couldn't go on.

So what is the purpose of being a user???
It's only part of the time that you don't feel
like a loser,

Or maybe not a loser but you just feel bad.
    You don't need drugs to keep from being
        depressed and sad.

Jenny, Jeff, Mike, and Ashley didn't think this
        way, though,
    They used more and more to stay on the go.

They had to be on something, so they could
        survive,
    But you know medically this won't keep you
        alive.

But still, everyone needs some kind of release,
    So that they can have a mind that is at
        peace.

They are, in a way, at peace now.
    Let me tell you how.

Their hearts are still cold and heavy as lead,
    But the only thing different now, is that
        they're dead.

This may shock you that I have written in this
        manner,
    I just don't want you to be served at death's
        dinner on drugs' silver platter.

Dear Ray,

I would like to thank you for sending me your
poem. Reading it was a moving experience. I was especially touched by how much you cared about your
friends. I can only begin to imagine the sadness you
experienced as you witnessed their self-destructive use
of drugs. But I am also impressed that you show such
insight into why students do drugs. Since you are so

insightful, I thought it might be a good idea for us to look at your poem again and talk about it.

Ray, I thought that your four friends, Jenny, Mike, Jeff, and Ashley, were living examples of what is happening to millions of students in their own homes. Jenny had low self-esteem because her parents told her terrible things about herself and after awhile she believed them. Mike's parents also hurt him deeply. They not only got a divorce, but then wanted Mike to pick one parent over the other. As you said in your poem, all that trauma in his family made poor Mike confused and sick. Then there's Ashley and Jeff. Their parents had either left or were dead.

These students were put into awful situations that forced them to fend for themselves long before they were really ready to. Ray, you are right, the pressures on your friends were unreal. Unfortunately, there are thousands of teenagers who have to live in nightmares like these every day. Worse yet, their situations aren't their only problem. As you so clearly put it, "It's as though the devil is making sure you are constantly taunted." I have come to the conclusion that Satan and his demonic forces are going full throttle to destroy the lives of kids. He must realize that Jesus is coming soon and that the end of his power over us is near. Therefore, he wants to take as many teenagers with him as possible when the ultimate end comes. He knows that if he can keep a teenager's mind away from God he has won a great victory. Yes, Ray, your former friends were taunted by Satan, the same Satan the Bible calls a liar and a destroyer.

Sometimes it is difficult for adults to understand why kids would turn to something as destructive as drugs. But there is a sad logic to it that makes it seem like the right thing to do. I thought you did a tremendous job of explaining this kind of logic in your poem:

> They all turned to something that wasn't in their
> plans.
> It was drugs, their only way out.
>   Drugs made them feel better without a doubt.
> Can't you understand the actions they have
> chosen?!!
>   Their lives miserable and wrecked, full of
>   mental erosion.
> Some of the things they've had to endure,
>   A million men couldn't handle, and that's for
>   sure.
> So they started a new life of drug use,
>   That shut away all their horrible abuse.

I agree with you. Most students don't start out saying, "I want to do drugs." I don't think they ask, "How can I do drugs?" Instead, they ask, "How can I stop my awful pain?" I think students hurt so much that they simply lose their perspective on how best to deal with their struggles. Then someone comes along and says to them, "Would you like to feel better? Drugs will make you feel better." Once they fall for that lie, they begin to believe that drugs are the only answer to their problems. As you said in your poem: "It was drugs, their only way out. / Drugs made them feel better without a doubt."

You may recall that former first lady Nancy Reagan started the antidrug program "Just Say No." The idea behind that program was for students to just say no to

anyone who offered them drugs. I'm sure Nancy
Reagan was sincere in trying to help kids get off drugs.
But what the program failed to understand was just
how hard it is to say no to drugs, especially if you think
those drugs will take away the pain—pain so bad that
you described it as something "A million men couldn't
handle." It's not as though your friends were dumb;
they "were once wonderful people with wonderful
minds." But people can't live without hope, and so
when all other hope was gone, they put their hope in
drugs.

I think that most students know that drugs are a
bad way to go. I think you explained the failure of drugs
extremely well:

> Though it seemed that when they were on a trip
>   their problems were gone,
>   They would come back down and still feel as if
>   they couldn't go on.
> So what is the purpose of being a user???
>   It's only part of the time that you don't feel
>   like a loser,
> Or maybe not a loser but you just feel bad.
>   You don't need drugs to keep from being
>   depressed and sad.

I also thought you did a great job when you explained how taking drugs is a cruel hoax. To begin with,
drugs only seemed to make their problems go away. But
of course that was just an illusion. Their problems were
still very much with them. Once they came off their
drug experience they still felt "as if they couldn't go
on." Not only were their problems still staring them in

the face, but they were also left craving a drug "high." Drugs created a longing in your friends that could only be fulfilled when they were high. Thus, when they were sober, they were miserable. Yes, Ray, you very clearly uncovered the lie of drug abuse: "It's only part of the time that you don't feel like a loser."

I think the message of your poem comes through loud and clear. "You don't need drugs to keep from being depressed and sad." It's too bad that millions of students haven't figured that out yet. And many are heading for the ultimate disaster that you referred to as you talked about the tragedy of your friends.

Your four friends got caught in a fatal trap. They were faced with a simple choice. They could either stay high and eventually die or be sober and miserable. They obviously chose to use "more and more to stay on the go." Physically, their bodies could not handle that kind of chemical abuse. In the end, something had to give. As you put it, "They had to be on something, so they could survive, / But you know medically this won't keep you alive." In the end the drugs, which they thought were helping them, killed them. Your friends were looking for life. Instead, they found death.

Ray, I agree with just about everything you said in your poem, and you said it far better than I ever could. There's just one line that I take issue with. Speaking of their death you said, "They are, in a way, at peace now." If your four friends never gave their lives to Christ, they are not at peace. They have learned the horrible errors of their ways. They must spend an eternity apart from Christ with only their painful regrets and no drugs to help them. It is an overwhelming tragedy that they never turned to the One who could truly help them. Jesus says in the Book of John,

> **I leave you peace; my peace I give you. I do not give it to you as the world does. So don't let your hearts be troubled or afraid.**
>
> **John 14:27**

Thank you again, Ray, for sending me your powerful poem. I believe it will help many students avoid the tragedy of drug abuse.

Your friend,
Dawson

5

Teenage Pregnancy

"I got involved with a guy
that I thought loved me
as much as I loved him.
Well, I got pregnant and
the love wasn't there,
neither was he."
—Ginger

WHEN I'M TEACHING THE SUBJECTS OF DATING AND SEX, I like to use the line, "If you play with the instruments, you'll get music." Sexually speaking, the American teenager is playing with the instruments, but the music they're getting is the blues. It's a sad, sad song that most of them never expected to hear. The statistics speak for themselves:

- Over 1 million teenagers will get pregnant this year; that's an average of roughly three thousand each day.
- One of every nine teenage women will become pregnant this year.
- Nearly 50 percent of these girls will end their pregnancies through abortion.

This is one of the most dreadful feelings a teenager can experience—the terror of finding out you're pregnant or that you've gotten someone pregnant. It is terrifying because there is no easy way out of the problem. There are some mistakes students make where they suffer few consequences, but teenage pregnancy is not one of them.

I am convinced that, outside of sexual abuse, there is nothing that frustrates a youth counselor more than having to deal with an unwanted pregnancy. There is very little a counselor, friend, or parent can do to ease the pain. However, one bad decision does not mean a student has to make another. In this chapter you'll see letters from a girl and a boy. Ginger and Mike are both painfully aware that they have made a mistake. Their greatest desire is to face that mistake and fix it. As you will see, I am painfully honest with them, but do my best not to condemn.

A Letter from Ginger

Dear Dawson,

I don't even know where to begin. See, my parents split up a long time ago—both of them have remarried now. My natural father has never cared for me. My stepmom and I hate each other. My natural mother and I didn't talk much, and my stepdad only says anything when he wants to yell at me. Well, I got involved with a guy that I thought loved me as much as I loved him. Well, I got pregnant and the love wasn't there, neither was he. I told my natural father and all he said was "get support from the father, not me." The news hit my stepmom and she said, "You made your bed, sleep in it." My stepdad wouldn't talk for weeks, then he said, "I'll adopt it." My natural mother responded with, "I'll set a doctor's appointment, we'll fix the problem before the whole town knows." I wouldn't go get an abortion, and now people tell me how stupid and low I am. My principal at school thinks I ought to drop out because it's not right for a girl to be pregnant and go to school. Would I have been a better person if I had an abortion? Well, my problems just started. I'm having a baby, the father won't look at me and my parents won't help me unless I sign papers for them to adopt the baby. I was going to over-dose, while everyone was asleep so nobody could take me to the hospital. I turned your show, "Too Young to Die" on accidentally. It wasn't planned. In fact, that was the night I planned to do the overdose—obviously I didn't do it. But now I am going to work out my problems—not run from them. But I do have one major problem ahead of me, this baby. I can't support it, but I don't want to give it up. I can't look for help in the father—he's too unstable. I guess I'll have to sign papers and live with that. I just really wrote to say "Thank You" for that show. Not only did it cause me to stop and think about my life, but my baby's life too. (The baby is due in November.) I gave myself another chance, and my baby a chance to know that life has its ups and downs—the ups are yet to come.

> Thanks a lot,
> Ginger

Dear Ginger,

Thank you for taking the time to write me your letter. You definitely have some serious problems. Getting pregnant outside of marriage can create a lot of complications, and you have your share of them. You face a number of very hard decisions. As you face these decisions, I want you to repeat this statement to your-self: Even though I made one mistake, it doesn't mean I have to keep making other mistakes. You have already had to face some incredibly tough choices. And based on what you have told me in your letter, you have made good choices. I can't begin to tell you how proud of you I am for this.

For example, you did not make the horrible mistake of committing suicide. Suicide is never a right choice. It is always wrong. I hope you can see that God was showing His love for you when He lead you to watch our television show, "Too Young to Die." He kept you from killing yourself because He knew that, with His help, you could face your problems. Of course, killing yourself would have also meant killing your baby. That would have been a double disaster. God knew that Satan would like nothing better than to destroy both you and your baby in one blow. And, Jesus warns us about Satan's destructiveness.

A thief comes to steal and kill and destroy, but I came to give life—life in all its fullness.
John 10:10

The Bible calls Satan a thief. He wanted to take something from you that didn't belong to him—the lives of you and your baby. He knows how special both of you are to God. However, God's gift to you was Jesus Christ. He loves you and wants both you and your child to have a life that is full of meaning, love, and purpose. Thus, He has done two things for you. He has stepped in and kept you from killing yourself, and He has of-fered you a life worth living.

You could have also made another terrible mistake. You could have listened to your natural mother and gone ahead and had an abortion. You wisely under-stood that an abortion might "fix" some problems, like embarrassment, but cause many, many more. God hates abortion. Down deep you clearly understood that it is taking the life of an innocent baby. It's not the baby's fault that you got pregnant. To kill an innocent child because its mother made a wrong choice is an even worse choice. I am very proud of you. Even though you faced a lot of pressure to have an abortion, you still made the right choice. Your choice must have also pleased God. In Psalm 139, the Bible clearly teaches that He is actively involved in creating a person even before that person is born.

> **For you created my inmost being;**
> **you knit me together in my mother's**
> **womb.**
> **My frame was not hidden from you**
> **when I was made in the secret place.**
> **When I was woven together in the depths of**
> **the earth,**
> **your eyes saw my unformed body.**
> **All the days ordained for me**
> **were written in your book**
> **before one of them came to be.**
>
> **Psalm 139:13, 15–16** NIV

Ginger, I know it's hard to carry a baby to full term when so few people are supporting you. However, you should be encouraged in a couple of ways. Be encouraged that you have done what is right. In addition, be encouraged that God has already made good plans for you and your baby. He loves to do good things for us when we are obedient. The people that tell you how stupid you are for not getting an abortion are wrong.

They are only showing you how troubled, confused, selfish, and cold they have become toward life and toward God. You, on the other hand, have already shown that you care about what is right, and that you know how to make good decisions. Having an abortion may very well have crushed you emotionally. You would have had to live with the belief that you murdered your own baby. For some people, these thoughts haunt them for years and years. Thank God that you did not choose abortion as a quick fix for your problem. You will never have to live with horrible memories like those.

Ginger, I'm sorry that you got yourself pregnant. That was obviously a bad mistake. But then you stopped to think. You stopped making mistakes. You started making wise decisions. I couldn't be more proud of you. As I say to teenage women across America, "If you ever get pregnant out of wedlock, suicide and abortion are never an option." When you got pregnant, you were afraid, you felt unloved, and you were being pressured to do the wrong thing. Nevertheless, you said no to suicide and no to abortion. So far you have made the very best of a bad situation. The question is, where do you go from here?

Your next decision is whether to keep the baby and raise it yourself, or give it to someone else to raise. After reading your letter, I'm not sure that keeping your child is a good idea. I can think of four things that are working against you. First, you are very young. Raising a baby is a tremendous responsibility and is not easy, even when you are older. Second, you have your own deep emotional needs working against you. Right now you are barely able to function as a teenager from a severely broken home. Adding the pressure of providing for and taking care of the baby would probably be too much for you to bear. If you get overstressed you will eventually take it out on your child. This would make you feel guilty and only add pain for both of you. Third, in order to raise a baby at your age you would need a tremendous amount of support from your family. Obviously, the members of your family are not providing that support. Finally, you have said that your baby's father is "too unstable." If he is unstable, he could wind up causing you and the baby all kinds of problems. You need to do your best to provide your child with a good home to grow up in. It is difficult for me to say this, and even more difficult for you to hear it, but I don't think it would be fair to either you or the baby to keep and raise the baby yourself.

Your second choice is to allow the baby to be raised by your stepfather and your real mom. You must ask yourself, "Do they really want the baby?" Your real mother is the one who wanted you to have an abortion. It doesn't sound as if she really wants the baby. You said in your letter that your "stepdad wouldn't talk for weeks, then he said, 'I'll adopt it.'" The fact that he wouldn't talk to you for weeks indicates that he made a decision to adopt the baby out of desperation rather than out of love and commitment. It doesn't sound to me like your stepfather and natural mom really want this baby. In my opinion, at the present time, your mom and stepfather would not be able to provide the healthy, loving environment your child needs. And believe me, your child deserves a healthy, loving environment.

Your best choice is to give the baby up for adoption to a Christian couple. There are thousands of Christian couples who, for whatever reason, can't have children and are waiting to adopt a baby like yours. They would provide your child with the kind of love and support that it needs and deserves.

I think you also have one more choice concerning yourself. You need to get out of your chaotic home and into a Christian home for unwed mothers. You need to do this soon. There are many of these homes that would be willing to take you in. A home like this would provide you with physical, emotional, and spiritual support during this trying time and would help you locate a strong Christian family who would be willing to adopt your baby. I know it will be very difficult to give up your baby for adoption. However, you have already made some hard decisions, and you have made them well. Giving up your child to be raised by a godly family is an ultimate act of love. Your reward will be to know that your child is being greatly loved and well cared for.

Ginger, it's time for you to get on with your life. It was a miracle that you watched our television special "Too Young to Die." It was a miracle that God, through that show, kept you from killing yourself. But I think it's also miraculous that you wrote this letter and that you waited for this response. I know that everything seems dark now, but that darkness will pass. God loves you and your unborn child. He wants to give both of you a great future. He said, in Psalm 34,

> The LORD hears good people when they cry
> out to him,

> and he saves them from all their troubles.
> The LORD is close to the brokenhearted,
> and he saves those whose spirits have
> been crushed.
>
> Psalm 34:17–18

I will be praying that your decisions will be the right ones, and that they will bring honor to you, to your baby, and to God.

Your friend,
Dawson

A Letter from Mike

Dear Dawson,

I am a seventeen-year-old guy who knows that the Lord is the only way. Six and a half months ago I slept with a girl who is now six-and-a-half-months pregnant. Dawson, please tell all of the young men out there one more time to just wait. Because for me it was only a one night stand. Your one warning might be the one that keeps them out of the same situations that I'm in. Sometimes the shame is almost unbearable yet the Lord always seems to pull me through.

Sincerely,
Mike

Dear Mike,

Thank you for the brief but honest note that you have sent me. I also thank you for the simple plea that you have given me as to what to say to other guys. To begin with, I am really sorry that you have gotten your-self into this mess. I know that you are sorry, too, and have had some sleepless nights over all this. It truly is a guy's nightmare to find out that he has gotten some girl pregnant. Something you said in your note got my attention. You said, "It was only a one night stand." It's amazing how one wrong decision—one night with one girl—could cause so much hurt to so many. The hurt is not only for you but for this girl and the baby and all the people who know you both. Thinking about your wrong decision on that night reminds me of a simple verse in Ecclesiastes.

> **Dead flies will cause even a bottle of per-fume to stink! Yes, a small mistake can outweigh much wisdom and honor.**
>
> **Ecclesiastes 10:1** TLB

You ask me to do something for you and for all the other guys who are out there. You said, "Please tell all of the young men out there one more time to just wait." Mike, I want you to know that I will do that for you, for them, and for God. As you know, when it comes to the misuse of sex, in all of American history there has never been a generation more tempted than yours. Your generation has been told so many lies about sex and how great it is to have sex whenever you want. There-fore, it takes real commitment from guys to wait until marriage to have sex.

It takes commitment to God. A person must honor God and His Word completely in order to remain a virgin until he gets married. It also takes a strong com-mitment to all the women that the guy dates. He must be committed to not causing them pain, guilt, disappointment, and unwanted pregnancy and committed to helping protect them from disobeying God and hurting others. And it takes a commitment to one's self. The person must be committed not to abuse his own body for just a few moments of simple pleasure. We must realize that our bodies are temples to the Holy Spirit, and they are not to be trashed. There are tremendous rewards for those who are willing to make the heavy commitment to wait for marriage before having sex.

Mike, you were not willing to wait. You were not willing to make that commitment and, as you said, you are paying a real price. As you put it, "Sometimes the shame is almost unbearable yet the Lord always seems to pull me through." I want to encourage you, Mike. You made a mistake, but you still have a great future ahead of you. God sees that you are sorry for your sin against Him and He has forgiven you. Now God wants to work with you and help you face the consequences of your sin. Day by day His mercy and strength will be with you. In Psalm 103, King David, who also faced some horrible consequences for his sin in the area of sex, wrote this:

> **The LORD shows mercy and is kind. He does not become angry quickly, and He has great love. He will not always accuse us, and he will not be angry forever. He has not punished us as our sins should be punished; he has not repaid us for the evil we have done. As high as the sky is above the earth, so great is his love for those who respect him. He has taken our sins away from us as far as the east is from west. The LORD has mercy on those who respect him, as a father has mercy on**

his children. He knows how we were made; he remembers that we are dust.

Psalm 103:8–14

I hope your letter will get the attention of guys who think that they can fool around and not get burned. When we violate God's principles in some way or the other, we always get burned. I just wish every teenage guy in America could talk with you about these things. Mike, you warn as many guys as possible, and I will do the same. Perhaps, through God's help, we can save others from going through the needless pain you are experiencing.

Your friend,
Dawson

6

Sexual Abuse

"My father raped me.
My own biological father,
the one person I held
dearest in my life."
—Mary

IN THE SECOND HALF OF THIS CENTURY a shocking trend has occurred. As a nation, it has to be one of our worst nightmares come true. It is called sexual abuse, but somehow that name doesn't seem strong enough. It is the repulsive act of forcing sex on the young, the innocent, the helpless. Those who need and deserve protection the most, our children and teenagers, are being horribly violated by the very people who are supposed to be their protectors. What a horrendous perversion of trust!

Just how big is the problem of sexual abuse in our country?

- It is now estimated that one in five girls and one in seven guys will be abused by a relative before age eighteen.
- Each day, seven hundred young people are victimized by some type of sexual abuse.
- Most experts believe that sexual abuse against the young will continue to increase.

I want to say more about this last point. Not long ago, I was reading a little booklet called *Renewed Hope*

106

for Victims of Sexual Abuse by Robert McGee. McGee's organization, Rapha, has had a great deal of experience in helping sexual abuse victims recover. In this booklet, McGee clearly explained why he believed there will be an increase in sexual abuse in the future.

Sexual abuse will probably increase in the future because of several factors. First, child pornography is a growing industry and plays a major role in reducing people's sexual inhibitions. This, in turn, increases the likelihood that they will sexually abuse others. Second, the number of step-families, in which a child is eight times more likely to be abused, is also increasing. Seventeen percent of those raised by a stepfather will be abused before the age of fourteen, as opposed to only two percent of the women raised by a biological father.

Finally, the numbers of untreated childhood sexual abuse victims may contribute to a growth in sexual abuse cases. Reports indicate that 46% of the imprisoned sex offenders who show a persistent, exclusive preference for children were, themselves, sexually molested as children. In one treatment program for compulsive sexual behavior, 83% reported being victims of sexual abuse. Since these people are not receiving adequate treatment, they may continue to victimize others in the future.

The thought of sexual abusers multiplying throughout our nation is terrifying. I cannot imagine the humiliation and the sense of helplessness that these young people must feel when they are violated. The emotional damage is immense. Victims are left with feelings of shame, rage, fear, distrust, and confusion. These are deep scars on the soul that can't be fixed with a couple of counseling sessions. In some cases, it takes years for sexual abuse victims to put their lives back together.

Can God heal the wounds of the sexually abused? Yes, of course. God can do anything but fail. But this is where the Church of Jesus Christ must get involved. We must take an active role in helping the sexually abused get over what has happened to them. With loving patience, determination, and the awesome power of God, sexual victims can win a total victory over their traumatic past.

In this chapter you'll read a letter from Mary. It is a short letter, but it is laced with rage and confusion. If you have been a victim of sexual abuse, past or present, I hope my response to Mary will help you face your situation and reach out for help. If you think you know victims of sexual abuse, reach out to them. You may be their only lifeline.

A Letter from Mary

Dear Dawson McAllister,

Hi, my name is Mary. I'm sixteen years old and I have a question for you. How do you forgive someone who is the person you held the highest respect for? And yet that person you respect so much, my father, raped me. My own biological father, the one person I held dearest to my heart. My father and my youth pastors were the highest level in my life. I practically worshiped them. The lower levels were my mother. When I was two my real mother, who is now dying of AIDS, divorced my father. All my life I was fed a bunch of B.S. about her. I have one question that I don't have the answer to: Why should I forgive and forget what he did when he raped me? To tell you the truth, I hope he burns in Hell. I know that is pretty heavy, but that's just the way I feel. I don't understand. He didn't love me for me, he only wanted my body. My father didn't care for me, me—the person, he only wanted my body so he could get his jollies and people expect me to forgive and forget. And with my mom, I've grown up with either myself as a mom or my step-mom. As it turned out I hated her for taking the place of my real mother. I mean it's like my real mother didn't love me. Am I that horrible and bad? Please help me, you have answers. I'm confused and scared and don't know what to do. Here is a poem I wrote about my life. Please understand what I mean.

Daddy's Prostitute

She's sweet sixteen with a dark dark past
She's daddy's little prostitute. . . . She's his
        little whore
Who's just been kicked right out the door
He uses and abuses her to get his thrills at
        night
Maybe they were right, you're not much of
        anything
You're Daddy's little prostitute,
His private little whore.
People say he's great.
People say he's liked,
But I see the mask he wears.
I see the games he plays.
I'm sick and tired of the game.
I'm sick and tired of the pain.
I hate to be a player in this game of Charades
Because I'm Daddy's little

prostitute . . . Daddy's little whore
Who's on the verge of being kicked out the door.

> Please help me, I'm
> confused!
> Mary

Dear Mary,

I've had a chance to read your letter several times. It is one of the most difficult letters I have ever read. I can't begin to tell you how sorry I am that you have been a victim of such a vicious crime. When I think of some of the worst things that could happen to a child or a teenager, sexual abuse ranks right up there at the top. I just want you to know that I am shocked and saddened that this had to happen to you. I feel like David must have felt when he wrote,

> **Burning indignation has seized me because
> of the wicked,
> Who forsake Thy law.**
>
> **Psalm 119:53** NASB

Mary, there's no use in beating around the bush about your problem. Sexual abuse causes more pain and is harder to get over than almost anything that could happen to a teenager. It creates shame, rage, fear, confusion, a sense of helplessness, and certainly low self-esteem. You will have to face these emotions in order to fully recover. But remember, in the midst of your awful situation, God is there. Getting over what has happened to you will be a long, tedious journey. But it is a journey you can, and must, take.

110

I know you must sometimes feel so alone and beaten down that you can't go on. Don't give in to those feelings. You must go on. There is light at the end of your dark tunnel. King David, no doubt, felt much the same way as you do when evil people tried, in some way, to abuse him. Yet he knew that there was hope, even in his darkest hour. He said,

> **Do not hand me over to my enemies,**
> **because they tell lies about me**
> **and say they will hurt me.**
> **I truly believe**
> **I will live to see the LORD's goodness.**
> **Wait for the LORD's help.**
> **Be strong and brave,**
> **and wait for the LORD's help.**
>
> **Psalm 27:12–14**

I know you're in a dark hole right now, but God is with you. As painful as it is, you will get over this terrible predicament. Don't stop looking to God for hope. He will not let you down. With this important truth in mind, let's look at the things you are struggling with.

Sexual abuse victims nearly always feel a terrible sense of shame. It is very clear that you also feel this way. It's like having a gigantic scar that covers both your body and your soul. You are convinced that it's there for the whole world to see. It seems as if it will never fade away. You're left feeling alone, vile, and completely trashed. In your own mind you may feel you are the scum of the earth. Those seem to be the feelings

you were trying to express in your poem when you
wrote, "She's sweet sixteen with a dark dark past /
She's daddy's little prostitute. . . . She's his little
whore / Who's just been kicked right out the door."

Mary, you asked a very pointed question in your
letter. I want to answer that question right now. You
asked, "Am I that horrible and bad?" The answer to
your question is no, definitely not! What happened to
you sexually does not make you horrible and bad, it
makes you a victim. A victim is someone who cannot
stop what is happening to her. Your father has such
power over you and has violated you so often that you
have been helpless to stop him. Mary, I want you to
stop right now and repeat this to yourself: "I'm not
horrible and bad. I am a victim." I want you to repeat
this to yourself over and over again until you begin to
accept it as the truth.

If being a victim makes someone horrible and bad,
then Jesus would have been the worst. The Bible tells us
that He was sinless, and yet there has never been anyone more abused than He. In fact, I think that, when
Jesus hung on the cross, He was, in a sense, sexually
abused. Mary, I believe that as Jesus hung there He was
stripped naked for all the world to see. He was also
physically abused. He was so horribly beaten that He
was barely recognizable as a human. When Jesus hung
on the cross He felt more shame than you and I have
ever felt. At the crucifixion, Jesus not only took the
abuse of those who were staring and laughing at Him,
but He also took on the sins and the shame of the whole
world. He hated the shame He experienced. As the Bible
tells us,

> . . . fixing our eyes on Jesus, the author and per-
> fecter of faith, who for the joy set before Him en-
> dured the cross, despising the shame, and has sat
> down at the right hand of the throne of God.
>
> Hebrews 12:2 NASB

The point is this: Because Jesus has taken our abuse
on Himself, He has suffered every kind of embarrassing
abuse there is. And yet, He is fully loved by God and
sits at His right hand forever. Like Jesus, God loves you.
He does not see you as trash. Instead, if you have asked
Christ into your life, He has declared you as pure as He
is. In Christ, He sees you as His pure and wonderful
daughter whom He loves more than you and I could
ever imagine.

Mary, let me deal with another issue in your letter.
You said that your real mother left you when you were
just two years old. That is a very sad thing. I know this
has left you feeling abandoned, unloved, and most of
all, angry. It is easy for you to hate your mother and to
want to punish her. But God wants you to know that
you do not make a very good judge. You don't even
begin to know how to punish your mother. God said,

> My friends, do not try to punish others when
> they wrong you, but wait for God to punish them
> with his anger. It is written: "I will punish those
> who do wrong; I will repay them," says the Lord.
> But you should do this:
>   "If your enemy is hungry, feed him;
>   if he is thirsty, give him a drink.
>   Doing this will be like pouring burning
>   coals on his head."

Do not let evil defeat you, but defeat evil by doing good.

Romans 12:19–21

You have said that your mother is dying of AIDS. She is already going through a lot of suffering. Here is my advice to you. First, get some counseling. Then, go and find your mother and make peace with her before she dies. It will be difficult to do, but it will also bring you healing. You already have a heavy load to carry right now. You don't need to add to it with a destructive load of anger toward your mother. Besides, dying of AIDS is a terrible way to die. I'm quite sure that your mother is sorry for the selfish, irresponsible mistakes she has made in her life. As she faces death, at least you can help her by letting her know that she has made peace with her daughter. You may not be able to go and see your mother today. You may have to go down your own road to recovery for a while before you are able to do this. But my prayer for you is that she will live long enough for the two of you to make peace.

And now let's talk about someone who has caused even more pain for you. Let's talk about your father. To put it mildly, this man has truly violated you. He has hurt you in ways that only God can fully comprehend. In your letter you make it no secret that you are enraged toward him. You said, "Why should I forgive and forget what he did when he raped me? To tell you the truth I hope he burns in Hell. I know that is pretty heavy but that's just the way I feel." Anger is a natural response for what your father has done to you. Feeling angry is not bad, it is just an emotion that tells us there is a deep wound in our soul. It's when we act out our anger that we grieve

114

God and hurt ourselves and others. The Bible says,

> **When you are angry, do not sin, and be sure to stop being angry before the end of the day. Do not give the devil a way to defeat you.**
> **Ephesians 4:26–27**

This verse tells us not to spend too long being angry. Eventually, we must move on to forgiveness. What does it mean to be able to forgive your dad? It does not mean that you must forget how he has abused you. There is no way that you will be able to forget all the things he has done to you. However, in time, God in his goodness will take away the horrible feelings that go with those memories. There will come a time when you will still remember the awful things your dad did, but you will no longer have the negative emotions. You may see pictures in your mind, but you'll no longer experience the feelings that go with those pictures.

First, forgiving your father does not mean you should keep what he has done to you a dark family secret. You must bring what he has done to you to the light. Several lines in your poem make it clear that you've had enough of the lies. You wrote, "People say he's great. / People say he's liked, / But I see the mask he wears. / I see the games he plays. / I'm sick and tired of the game. / I'm sick and tired of the pain. / I hate to be a player in this game of Charades." God never intended for you to be part of a cover-up to this kind of treacherous abuse. This kind of secret will only make you suffer more. You need to tell your story to people you can trust. And then you need to begin seeing a counselor. You will be amazed at how much better you will feel once you start getting the support that you need. It will be very difficult and embarrassing to disclose what has happened to you. But remember, it did not happen because you did something wrong. Your father is the one who committed the crime. You were but a victim. It was your father's sin. He, and only he, is responsible. Whatever happens to your family or to your father is his responsibility.

Second, forgiving your dad does not mean you should protect him from punishment. He has committed a crime for which he must answer. However, forgiving him does mean that you will not try to take personal vengeance upon him. It would be easy to want to make him pay, but like the situation with your mother, you need to let God deal with him. Matthew 18 tells us that God takes it very seriously when an adult violates a child.

> **But whoever causes one of these little ones who believe in Me to stumble, it is better for him that a heavy millstone be hung around his neck, and that he be drowned in the depth of the sea. "Woe to the world because of its stumbling blocks! For it is inevitable that stumbling blocks come; but woe to that man through whom the stumbling block comes!"**
>
> **Matthew 18:6–7** NASB

If I were you, Mary, I would pray that God would have mercy upon your father for what he has done to you. His sin against you and God is sure to cost him a very dear price. If you knew the punishment coming his way, it would probably cause you to pray twice as much on his behalf.

Finally, you must bring what your father has done to you to the light to save others from his crimes. I don't know whether or not you have other sisters, but most sexual abusers will strike again if they have the opportunity. And most sexual abusers will not face their menacing addiction until they are forced to. Your father is a very, very sick man caught in bondage from which he cannot escape by himself. I say this with a broken heart, but your father must be stopped. Only when he has had to face the consequences of his actions will he begin to get help, and only then can he hope to get well.

Mary, near the end of your letter said, "I'm confused and scared and don't know what to do." These feelings are totally understandable. However, before I end this letter, I want to be sure that we have cleared away the confusion about what you must do next. If you are to get out of your awful predicament and get on the road to recovery, then you must follow my directions.

First, you need to pray that God will help you to do what He wants you to do at this dark hour. Remember, He is with you. If you let Him, He will become more real to you at this time than you ever imagined. He tells us in the Bible that He wants to help us in times like these.

> **So don't worry, because I am with you. Don't be afraid, because I am your God. I will make you strong and will help you; I will support you with my right hand that saves you.**
>
> **Isaiah 41:10**

With God's help, the next thing you must do is go to the person that you trust the most. Perhaps it is your youth pastor or Sunday school teacher or a teacher at school. Whoever that person is, you must tell him or her the whole story. You must ask that person to help you find the appropriate people who will help you get out of that house and to a safe place where your father can't hurt you any more.

The third thing you must do is find a professional Christian counselor who specializes in dealing with sexual abuse victims. Your trusted friend can help you. And because God knows exactly what you need, I'm sure He already has an excellent counselor waiting— one who will love you and help you recover. However, you need to understand that this will not be a quick fix. There is a good chance that you will need long-term therapy. But no matter how long the road to recovery might be, you must stay with it. God will give you the strength to face whatever you must face. He loves you, and He is on your side. What has happened to you is a tragedy, but you will achieve victory over it. If you trust God and really want to get well, nothing can stop you. Mary, no matter how tough it gets, remember this message from Psalm 34:

> **The LORD hears good people when they cry out to him, and he saves them from all their troubles. The LORD is close to the brokenhearted, and he saves those whose spirits have been crushed.**
> **Psalm 34:17–18**

You are a good person, Mary, and God loves you very much.

Your friend,
Dawson

7

Verbal and Emotional Abuse

> "I tried to take
> my own life . . .
> because my parents
> kept telling me how
> worthless I was. . . ."
> —Heather

STICKS AND STONES CAN BREAK MY BONES, but words can never hurt me." Not only is the saying old, it simply isn't true. Words are powerful! A sharp tongue can inflict lasting damage. If you keep telling someone that he is no good, after a while he's going to believe it. It's true of adults, and it's definitely true of teenagers. In fact, a child who is verbally abused over a long period of time often feels so inadequate that he or she becomes suicidal. I believe that in all of history this generation of teenagers has been put down verbally more than any other. Studies now show that a million children suffer the consequences of verbal abuse each year.

- A recent study revealed that the average parents talk to their teen just fourteen minutes a day, but nearly twelve minutes of that time is "spite and fight" talk.
- 93 percent of all adolescents say that they have some serious communication breakdowns between themselves and their parents.

Though this introduction has been about verbal abuse, we really need to consider the larger category of emotional abuse. Emotional abuse includes negative words as well as actions that damage our spirits. It is often hard to identify a student who has been emotionally abused. However, there are certain symptoms in those who have been battered down which can be seen when we take a closer look. Most victims of emotional abuse lack self-confidence. They are usually withdrawn, though they can be angry or hostile. Emotionally abused students often lack the desire to succeed. They have been emotionally beaten down so much that they are afraid to try for fear that they will be beaten down again.

One such student is Heather. Her letter broke my heart. To the best of my knowledge she has never been physically abused. She does not come from a broken home. Yet the emotional abuse she has received from her parents has all but destroyed her. The two people God designed to nurture Heather have done incredible damage. Her self-esteem is in rubble. Her joy for life has long since been snuffed out. Of all the letters I've received, I found hers one of the most difficult to answer.

A Letter from Heather

Dawson,

My name is Heather. I am seventeen years old and am in desperate need of your help. Today in my Bible class, I saw one of your films (TV program) on suicide. About two months ago, I tried to take my own life by swallowing eighty sleeping pills. I did it because my parents kept telling me how worthless I was, and I had a feeling that my "friends" felt the same way, too. Unfortunately, one of my real friends found me before the drugs could do any real harm. She took me to a hospital where they pumped my stomach and made me throw up. I felt so humiliated. They then put me through a series of psychiatric programs. They didn't help. When I got home, my parents treated me like a princess. They did things for me to make up for the sixteen years of hell that they put me through. Then they turned against me again. They started telling me that I should have killed myself the first time, then they proceeded to show me the right way to slash my wrists. I felt as if they were laughing the whole time . . . like they wanted me to do it! Well, by then I had had it. So I took my parents' suggestion and tried to kill myself again, this time slashing my wrists . . . and again I failed. You see, I can't even kill myself the right way. I always end up messing it up somehow. What can I do now? I don't really want to die, I just want someone to love me. But there is no one. Not even God can help me. I became a Christian when I was ten years old, but things seem different now. I prayed for an answer from Him, but the one He gave me just made things worse. Did I just give up too easily? Where do I go now?

I still live with my parents, but they act like I'm not there. They say they won't waste money on a psychiatrist because they don't think I'm worth it. Am I? Sometimes I wonder. I'm not anything to them. Just a shadow on the wall. I feel like I am their problem, ever since I was born I have been. I do take a psychology class in school to try to understand myself, and they say that if you take up a hobby, it could relieve some pain. So I tried poetry. But that doesn't work either 'cause all I can come up with are really morbid poems.

PLEASE, IF YOU CAN . . . HELP ME!!!

—Heather

124

Dear Heather,

Every so often I get a letter from a student that knocks me off my feet. Your letter has done that. Every so often I get a letter that makes me angry at the way a teenager is being treated. The way you have been treated has made me angry. And yet, Heather, I want you to know that in spite of all the awful things that have happened to you, there is still hope. Even though you can see no way out of your predicament, there is a way out. So before you read any further, I want to tell you something. In fact, I want you to write it down. Then I want you to say it out loud. Okay, here it is: "Dawson says there's hope and I choose to believe him."

After reading your letter several times, I have come to this conclusion. I believe that you have been emotionally abused. This is very sad. However, there is something about your situation that is even worse. The saddest thing that has happened to you is that you have chosen to believe the abuse that has been dumped upon you. Because you constantly hear it, and because you have begun to believe it, you're feeling worthless, hopeless, and trapped. Heather, I'm sorry for what you have gone through, but I want you to know that it can change. You are not worthless. Your situation is not hopeless. With God's help, there is no such thing as a dead end.

First of all, you and I must sadly agree that your parents are troubled. I hate to have to say that to you, but for you to get well, you must first realize that some of your problems aren't your fault. Parents who tell their children they're useless are emotionally abusive parents. I don't know why your parents have done this to you. They are obviously angry. But no matter what has happened to them, there is still no excuse for their destructive behavior toward you. Perhaps in their own sickness they do not understand just how damaging their words really are. However, God does understand the power of words. He is very clear that our words can do horrendous damage. Look at what the Bible says about the words of a verbal abuser in Psalms.

> **They make their tongues sharp as a snake's;**
> **their words are like snake poison.**
> **Psalm 140:3**

Heather, many of the things your parents have said to you have acted on you just like snake poison. It is very clear that your spirit has been crushed by evil words. I was especially disturbed by your description of your parents' showing you how to kill yourself. My guess is that, at first, they felt guilty for the way they had treated you. They probably felt humiliated and helpless that you had to be "put through a series of psychiatric programs." Therefore, when you got home they wanted to treat you as well as possible. But after a while they became convinced that you weren't changing or getting better. They were already angry at you for attempting suicide the first time. Now they lost hope and became even angrier. In their rage, they suggested that you try to kill yourself again. I doubt that they really expected you to. They had simply let their anger and frustration overwhelm them. Your parents need deep spiritual and emotional help. They need to get to the bottom of their own destructive behavior.

But you do not have to let what your parents have done to you destroy you. You do not have to let their weaknesses keep you from getting well. God does not want you to be depressed or self-destructive. You can choose to live the way God wants you to live. I often say to students who have been abused, "It is not your fault that you are somebody else's victim; however, it is your responsibility to get well." You see, Jesus was also emotionally abused by others. He, too, had people who mocked Him and tried to hurt Him. But He refused to give up. The Bible talks about this in Hebrews.

> **Think about Jesus' example. He held on**
> **while wicked men were doing evil things to him.**
> **So do not get tired and stop trying.**
>
> **Hebrews 12:3**

Jesus endured abuse in order to show us that we could endure it, too. Jesus overcame abuse and had a productive life for God. He did this to show us that we could, too. Heather, I'm going to give you some ways you can get over the pain of being abused and get on with a productive life for God. As I share these ideas, I want you to keep Jesus' example firmly in your mind.

I believe that your main problem is that you have believed the abusive statements that have been thrown at you. You have allowed your parents' destructive words and actions to affect your emotions so deeply that they have changed the way you look at your entire life. This is not surprising. I believe that most abused people do the same thing. I want to refer back to your letter so that you can see just how seriously this abuse has affected you.

When you talked about why you swallowed the sleeping pills, you said, "I did it because my parents kept telling me how worthless I was, and I had a feeling that my 'friends' felt the same way, too." Heather, you are not worthless. However, because your parents have said you are worthless you now believe it. To believe that you are worthless is incredibly depressing. It almost destroys your ability to think straight. In your case, you convinced yourself of two things that were not true. First, you reasoned that if you were worthless to your parents, you must also be worthless to your friends. Then you reasoned that if your parents and friends felt that way, there was no use to go on living. Having lost all hope, you tried to kill yourself.

I'm glad you failed. Your reasoning was wrong. Just because your parents said you are worthless doesn't mean that you are worthless. I am convinced that you are more valuable than you have ever imagined. It is also very clear that your friends don't think that you are worthless. Wasn't it a friend who found you after you swallowed that deadly dose of pills? Did she tell you that you were worthless and just leave you to die? NO! She rushed you to the hospital because she never had a doubt that you are a very valuable person.

Heather, the first thing you need to do to get well is to quit believing the abusive things that your parents have said about you. I believe that the only way for you to be successful at this is by beginning to believe the good things that God has said about you. To replace old lies with new truths is not easy. Nevertheless, over time, and with God's help, it can be done. You see, our emotions come from our beliefs about ourselves. When we believe bad things about ourselves, it is only a small step to having feelings of self-hate and depression. On the other hand, when we start to believe that there is something good about ourselves, we will also start to feel good about ourselves.

I need to make something very clear. We should never depend on parents and friends to tell us what we are worth. As you already know, it is very depressing to hear hurtful things from them. It is also very encouraging to get praise and compliments from them. The problem is, they can easily change their minds. God does not change His mind. To find out what we are worth we must turn to Him, and Him alone. Let's look at what God says about us in Jeremiah 31.

I love you people with a love that will last forever.

Jeremiah 31:3b

I think this is amazing! God, in His perfect love and kindness, has never thought of you as worthless. He has never thought of you as trash. In fact, it is just the opposite. All day, all night, every day and every night, forever, He loves you!

And the book of Jeremiah is not the only place He tells about His love for you. Let's look at Isaiah 43.

. . . You are precious to me . . . I give you honor and love you.

Isaiah 43:4a

I know that you haven't felt loved. But God wants you to know that you are more than loved, you are precious to Him. You are so loved and honored by God that, in 1 Peter 1, He actually tells you that you are worth far more to Him than all the money in the world.

God paid a ransom to save you from the impossible road to heaven which your fathers tried to take, and the ransom he paid was not mere gold

or silver, as you very well know. But he paid for you with the precious lifeblood of Christ, the sinless, spotless Lamb of God.

1 Peter 1:18–19 TLB

Do you think God would send His only son, Jesus Christ, to earth to suffer the kind of death He suffered for someone who is worthless? NEVER! We are incredibly valuable to God. For us to believe that we are worthless is to insult Him. He is the one who knows all things. He is the one who can cut through the confusion of our emotions and the distortion of other people's lies and abuse. And He is the one who says we are priceless. You said in your letter, "I don't really want to die, I just want someone to love me." God doesn't want you to die, either. He loves you. He loves you. He loves you. You are His precious daughter, and in His eyes you are worth more than you and I can ever comprehend.

Heather, let's review the first thing you need to do to get well. You must stop believing the abusive things your parents have said about you and start believing the terrific things God has said about you.

Now let's look at what I believe is your second big problem. You are convinced that God does not have the power to help you. In your letter you said, "Not even God can help me. I became a Christian when I was ten years old, but things seem different now." Things may seem different to you now, but I assure you that God and His mighty power have not changed one bit. The Bible is clear that nothing is too difficult for God.

Oh, Lord GOD, you made the skies and the earth with your very great power. There is nothing too hard for you to do.

Jeremiah 32:17

When we become depressed, we almost always become confused about the truth of our situation. We tend to think that God is as weak as we are. We wrongly believe that since we can't figure a way out of our problem, He can't either. We mistakenly reason that if we are powerless to change our situation, God must be powerless, too. But, Heather, God already knows everything about your problems, and He already has a plan to rescue you from your hurts and fears. In fact, your situation is not worse than that of a man in the Old Testament named Job. His house was destroyed. His crops were ruined. His livestock was stolen. His children were killed. He developed boils all over his body. His friends came to him and tried to convince him that it was all his fault. And, last but not least, even his wife told him to "Curse God and die" (Job 2:9b NIV). In the middle of his situation, he, too, wondered if God had a plan for him. The good news is that even though he had to go through a terrible time of suffering, God did have a plan for him. Job not only came through his troubles stronger than ever, he also shared with us what he learned about God. He said,

> **I know that you can do all things and that no plan of yours can be ruined.**
>
> **Job 42:2**

If God could rescue poor Job from all his troubles and suffering, He can certainly do the same thing for you.

You ask two very important questions in your letter. Your first question was, "Did I just give up too easily?" With all the compassion in my heart I must answer you by saying yes. I know you have been hurt, and hurt deeply. However, you simply cannot allow yourself to stay in the depression you are now in. You must believe that God does love and cherish you. You must also believe that He has the power and a plan to help you get up and get well. You need to put in your heart the confidence that a young King David boldly stated in Psalm 18.

With your help I can attack an army. With God's help I can jump over a wall.

Psalm 18:29

To put it another way, you must do what the writer of Hebrews asks us to do when we feel weak and tired:

So take a new grip with your tired hands, stand firm on your shaky legs, and mark out a straight, smooth path for your feet so that those who follow you, though weak and lame, will not fall and hurt themselves, but become strong.

Hebrews 12:12–13 TLB

I know that you don't feel like you have any strength left. Yet, with God's help, there is a lot more strength left in you than you think. Heather, I want you to ask yourself this very important question, "If I don't make it my responsibility to trust God and get well, what will happen to me?" The answer to that question is—NOTHING GOOD!

In answering your second question, "Where do I go now?" I want to give you a few practical things you can do. To begin with, you must get back into counseling. A strong Christian counselor will help you deal with the effects of your emotional abuse and the effects of your two suicide attempts. You need someone to walk alongside of you and help you keep your eyes on Jesus while focusing on getting well. Ask your pastor or youth pastor to help you find a good counselor.

It would be my guess that this counselor will also help you work through your problems with your parents. In time, your parents will probably have to be brought into the counseling process. This will be painful, but you must have the courage to see these problems with your parents get solved.

Finally, I'm going to give you a new hobby to try. I want you to find all the verses in the Bible that talk about God's love and God's power. Perhaps your Bible teacher at your school will help you find all these verses. Then I want you to memorize them. As you go to sleep at night think about those verses. If you want to write poetry, write it about the truths in the verses you have memorized. This hobby will help you in two ways. First, it will help you get rid of all those lies and negative emotions in your heart. Second, it will help you learn how very much God loves you and wants to help you.

Heather, I want you to know that I think you are a wonderful person. I am convinced that you have tremendous worth. I would never have spent all this time writing a letter to a person I thought was worthless. But more important than what *I* think is what *God* thinks. He is not only convinced that you are an incredibly valuable person, but He knows that He has a great future planned for you. So get up and get well!

Your friend,
Dawson

P.S. Don't ever, ever, ever try to commit suicide again!

8

Occult Involvement

"I am an initiated witch.
I didn't sacrifice any
humans or animals . . .
but I have cast spells and
conjured up demons."
—Wendy

THERE IS NO QUESTION IN MY MIND THAT SATAN is out to destroy the American teenager. He knows that if he can cause students to turn away from Christ he has a very good chance of keeping them in the dark forever. Yet, as much as he hates teenagers, he also wants to be worshiped by them. This is nothing new. In the fourth chapter of Matthew we find him pleading with Christ to worship him. Christ, of course, was not fooled by Satan's cheap impersonation of God Almighty. Unfortunately, many students are.

There really aren't any reliable statistics on how many students are caught up in the occult. However, in my experience, I would say that Satan worship is definitely on the increase. Moreover, I'm convinced that most students who get involved in the occult have no idea what a horrible nightmare they are walking into. Most of them come from dysfunctional families. They are almost always starving for acceptance. They often see the occult as a way to experience power over their sad and empty lives. What they fail to understand is that the only power Satan gives to them is the power to destroy themselves and others.

Few students jump right into full-blown Satan worship. Normally, they begin by dabbling at the fringes. Playing occult games and becoming a fan of certain rock music bands are ways of dabbling. Unfortunately, far too many students (and one is too many) are drawn from this dangerous dabbling into destructive Satanic rituals themselves. They throw themselves into the arms of a counterfeit god hoping to find the love and acceptance that only the real God, Jesus Christ, can give.

In this chapter we'll look at the effects of Satanism on two different students. Wendy, who is about to be destroyed by Satan and his demonic forces, and Debbie, who has encountered demons but seems to have gotten victory over them.

When a student is involved in the occult, I take it very seriously. These students have become prisoners of the greatest enemy mankind has ever had. They are on the brink of disaster and need immediate help. Yet, we should have no lack of confidence. Our God is infinitely more powerful than Satan, and He is still in the business of rescuing teenagers, even teenagers trapped in the occult.

A Letter from Wendy

Dear Dawson,

I'm in serious trouble and can't seem to get out. I left the church. I was going back in January of this year. I thought I could handle things on my own. My relationship with my mother was going down hill. I was taking all my anger, frustration, and inability to cope with an absentee father out on her. She didn't deserve that, but I didn't care. I haven't seen my father since June 1991. I never got a call or anything on my birthday. I'm beginning to wonder if my father just doesn't love me anymore. I've yet to hear that man say he's proud of me. Little by little, any love I have for him is being eaten away by hurt and anger.

Then I moved out and moved in with Steven. Nothing sexual was going on. Here's my problem. Steven is some higher up warlock as well as a high priest in the Satanic church. At first, I was letting it go through one ear and out the other. But after continual dealings with my mother and people from church, I joined his coven. Yes, I am an initiated witch. I didn't sacrifice any humans or animals. I don't intentionally hurt people, but I have cast spells and conjured up demons. I'm not kidding!! But they've been "controlled" by Steven. The only things I've called up demons for is protection against angels. I can't explain what happened or how things happened. All I know is I want out, but something won't let me.

I have had people tell me that warlocks, witches, and demons don't exist. I always ask them, "What euphoric planet are you from?" These things are VERY REAL. This is not "playtime" anymore. If I don't get out soon, I don't know what I'll do.

My mom would put me out if she knew the whole story. I'm stuck in the mud and going down slowly. I need your help!

Sincerely,
Wendy

Dear Wendy,

I read your letter, and I agree with you. You are in serious trouble. In fact, I can't think of any trouble more serious than falling into the hideous grip of witchcraft and Satan worship. Unfortunately, more and more teenagers are experimenting with these things. Even Christian teenagers are getting caught up in them. This letter will be very direct because, as you put it, "These things are *very real*. This is not 'playtime' anymore."

In your letter you made the statement, "I can't explain what happened or how things happened." Before we go any further, you need to understand that Satan and his demons do have supernatural power. However, they use that power to trap us and destroy us. I believe that Satan especially hates teenagers. He knows that teenagers are the ones who are most likely to become Christians. I read somewhere that the average age for becoming a Christian is fifteen. Satan also knows that once teenagers believe in something they will go all out for it. Therefore, he especially hates Christian teenagers who are really living for Christ since they are actually robbing him of his kingdom. So you see, Wendy, Satan is out to destroy you because he wants to destroy all teenagers, but especially Christian teenagers. The Bible warns us about this in 1 Peter 5.

> **Be self-controlled and alert. Your enemy the devil prowls around like a roaring lion looking for someone to devour.**
>
> **1 Peter 5:8** NIV

Satan is the cruelest being who ever existed. Far too many students are already being devoured by his cruel and clever tricks. Yet, as powerful as he is, Satan can't just come in and devour someone at will. As the Bible says, he "prowls around like a roaring lion" looking for people who have left themselves unprotected to his attack. You have allowed yourself to become unprotected. You are vulnerable. Judging from your letter, you have let your anger and rage toward your father take control of your life. The Bible clearly teaches that when we let anger become the center of our life, we are giving Satan the opportunity to do us great damage.

> **When you are angry, do not sin, and be sure to stop being angry before the end of the day. Do not give the devil a way to defeat you.**
>
> **Ephesians 4:26–27**

Wendy, it is almost certain that your anger was one way Satan was able to get such a destructive grip on your life. Unfortunately, it seems as if you have given him some other opportunities, as well. You said in your letter, "I thought I could handle things on my own." This was definitely a mistake. People cannot handle things on their own. Jesus said,

> **I am the vine, and you are the branches. If any remain in me and I remain in them, then they produce much fruit. But without me they can do nothing.**
>
> **John 15:5**

When we try to face life on our own, without Christ helping and defending us, we become fair game to Satan's lies and power. People who think they are strong enough to live life on their own eventually find out that they are sadly mistaken. Sometimes they only find this out after they have done serious damage to their lives. What Jesus said is always true, without Him we can do nothing. When we are not walking with God, one mistake almost always leads to another.

I think you made another crucial mistake. To put it in your words, "I left the church." By leaving the church, you left behind the people who could best help to protect you from Satan and his demonic forces. Church is far more than a place where we go to hear sermons. It is a place where we meet with other Christians to encourage, confront, and love one another. The Bible talks about how important this is.

> **Let us think about each other and help each other to show love and do good deeds. You should not stay away from the church meetings, as some are doing, but you should meet together and encourage each other. Do this even more as you see the day coming.**
>
> **Hebrews 10:24–25**

I hope you can see how your mistakes made it much easier for Satan to get such a powerful grip in your life. You were angry at your dad. You thought you could handle things on your own. You left the church and the loving counsel of your mother. These three mistakes left you wide open to be wiped out. Like the prodigal son that Jesus talks about in Luke 15, you had no place to go but down.

Yes, Wendy, you threw the door of your life wide open to Satan, and he was ready when you did. Look who he sent your way. It wasn't just anyone; it was Steven, a Satan worshiper. Somehow you deceived yourself into thinking that as long as you didn't have sex with him, it was okay to live with him. However, Satan had far bigger plans for you than simply losing your virginity. His plan was to enslave you into the treacherous world of Satan worship. You must have been surprised that it took so little time for you to get caught up in this bondage. Nevertheless, here you are, held tight in the vicious grip of Satan and his demons. You said it yourself in your letter, "All I know is I want out, but something won't let me." You are trapped by a power that you can't control. You are all but overwhelmed by this horrible demonic oppression.

I am encouraged that you so clearly understand that Satan and demons are real. It's too bad that so many people don't. As you said in your letter, "I have had people tell me that warlocks, witches, and demons don't exist. I always ask them, 'What euphoric planet are you from?' These things are *very real*." Satan wants to fool people into thinking that he and his demon followers do not exist. Jesus knows this. That is why He so often taught about Satan and demons. Christ wants us to know what you have learned the hard way—that we are all caught up in a deadly war with spirits we cannot see.

Unfortunately, knowing that demons are real doesn't get you out of their grip. Your feelings of help-lessness came through loud and clear when you said, "If I don't get out soon, I don't know what I'll do." Wendy, if you don't get out, I do know what you will do. You'll slide farther and farther down the slippery path to destruction. I believe it is just a matter of time before Satan completely destroys you. In fact, this is what Jesus said about Satan.

A thief comes to steal and kill and destroy.
John 10:10

It's very simple. If you want to have your life completely destroyed, stay where you are. However, if you really want to get out, you can. Look at John 10:10 again, only this time let's include what Jesus said about Himself.

A thief comes to steal and kill and destroy.
But I came to give life—life in all its fullness.
John 10:10

Wendy, you ended your letter with a very dramatic appeal. You said, "I'm stuck in the mud and going down slowly. I need your help!" I believe you are sincere. I also believe that you are ready to do what you have to do to escape Satan's bondage. Here is my advice.

To begin with, you must call out to Jesus Christ and plead with Him to rescue you. I know you feel weak and lost. But you must turn to Christ with all the energy you can muster. Jesus said,

Come to me, all of you who are tired and
have heavy loads, and I will give you rest. Accept
my teachings and learn from me, because I am
gentle and humble in spirit, and you will find rest
for your lives. The teaching that I ask you to ac-
cept is easy; the load I give you to carry is light.
Matthew 11:28–30

I want to give you a prayer to pray to Christ right now. Remember, He is not nearly as concerned about your words as He is with the attitude of your heart.

Dear God,

I realize that I have sinned against you by becoming involved in Satan worship. Because of what Christ has done at the cross for me, I'm asking you to forgive me. In your power, I renounce my involvement with Satan at this very moment. I renounce the devil and his influence in my life by the power of the blood of Jesus Christ. I trust in Him as my only hope. Please, God, give me the power and determination to break away from Steven and all those involved in Satan worship. Please protect me from all demons and set me free from all of their power. With all that I am, Jesus, I call out to you for help. In Jesus' name, Amen.

You must immediately leave Steven and everyone involved in Satan worship. Don't plan good-byes or last-minute speeches. You have been a prisoner. A person planning an escape doesn't stop to say good-bye to his jailers. You must be prepared to leave everything behind. You must run away from those people as quickly as possible. In fact, you may want to call a Christian that you really trust and ask him or her to come and get you. But whatever you do, you must do it quickly. Leave at once!

Then you must run to the safety of people who really love Christ. You need to go back to the church that you left behind. The people who worked with you before you left will welcome you back with open arms. I doubt very much if your mom will put you out if you go home again. But even if she does, there is someone at the church who will take you. When you return to the Christians at your church, ask them to help you deal with any demons that still may be harassing you. Ask them to help you renounce anything in your life that has given Satan the opportunity to keep you in bondage.

After you have done all of these things, you need to submit yourself to long-term Christian counseling. You need to deal with the unresolved anger toward your father. If you don't, you will only be open to another attack by Satan.

Wendy, let me again impress upon you the terrible danger you are in. I'm pleading with you to follow the advice I have just given to you. I know you have the courage to do this. You have to. Your whole life depends upon it!

Your friend,
Dawson

A Letter from Debbie

Dear Dawson,

I wanted to talk to you about a couple of past experiences. I used to smoke and drink. I gave it up about a year ago. I'm fourteen years old, and I've had sex four times. I know God will forgive me, but, even so, I feel alone. At least that was how I felt until your youth conference last month in which you said a lot of things that touched me.

Ever since your conference I have had two visits by demons. The first one didn't tell me his name. Well, neither one did really. Anyway, the first time I could not see him, but I heard and felt him. He was telling me God didn't love me and that He didn't want me around. He was telling me that anyone I thought loved me really didn't. The demon started tugging on my arm to go with him. I told him to get out and leave me alone in the name of Jesus Christ, and he was gone. When the second demon came to me, I couldn't understand what he was saying. He had a green face with red streaks going down the sides and yellow eyes with a black dot between them. That's all I can remember. I'm scared. Please pray for me!

I'm scared, Help Me!

Love,
Debbie

Dear Debbie,

I read your letter about your encounter with demons. It sounds like a pretty wild story, but I happen to believe you. Jesus not only taught about demons but also dealt with them throughout His earthly ministry. These evil spirits are still at work today trying to stop the work of God. There are some Christians who believe that demons no longer exist. The Bible is clear that these Christians are wrong. Demons are alive, well, and active around the world. I also believe that as we get to the end of time, Satan and his demonic forces will work extra hard to fight against God. But, of course, they will never win.

I'm not really sure why it is these two demons are harassing you. I think we become more vulnerable to their attack when we openly sin against God. Maybe when you were drinking and having sex you somehow let yourself become more open to an attack. You mentioned at the end of your letter that you were scared. I want you to know that you don't have to be afraid of demons. God tells us that in His spirit we can have tremendous power and courage. The Bible talks about this in 2 Timothy.

> God did not give us a spirit that makes us afraid, but a spirit of power and love and self-control.

> 2 Timothy 1:7

There are several things you need to know about demons in order to get them out of your life. First of all, you need to understand that demons are liars. When they tell you that God doesn't love you and those around you don't love you, they are lying. Demons, like their leader Satan, are deceptive, subtle, and full of clever lies. Even Christians can be harassed and confused by them. The Bible talks about this in 1 Timothy.

> Now the Holy Spirit clearly says that in the later times some people will stop believing the faith. They will follow spirits that lie and teachings of demons.

> 1 Timothy 4:1

If this demon should ever talk to you again, be assured that most, if not all, of what he is saying to you is false.

The second thing you need to know is that with Christ's power, demons will flee from you. You have already experienced this power. You said in your letter, "The demon started tugging on my arm to go with him. I told him to get out and leave me alone in the name of Jesus Christ, and he was gone." The key is to be so submitted to God that when the demons look at you they see Jesus. Demons are terrified of Jesus. Satan himself must run from us when, empowered by God, we stand against him. The Bible talks about this, too.

So give yourselves completely to God. Stand against the devil, and the devil will run from you.
James 4:7

As you are starting to understand, Debbie, there is tremendous power in the person of Christ. Jesus said,

All power in heaven and earth is given to me.
Matthew 28:18

If you keep being committed to God and claiming the power of the person of Christ when they attack, they will be forced to leave. Here is something else you need to know. Demons hate to hear about the cross of Jesus and the blood that was shed for our sins. The Bible says, in Revelation,

And our brothers and sisters defeated him by the blood of the Lamb's death.
Revelation 12:11a

What I would suggest you do is to find several verses that talk about the death of Christ. When you sense these evil spirits are near you need to read them. You may also want to get some "praise tapes" ready to play in your tape recorder. Demons hate praise to God. They don't like to be around when praise is being sung.

Just remember, Debbie, that you have great authority in Christ and can command these demons to leave and they must. In fact, I want to leave you with this simple prayer you can pray when you sense you are being demonically attacked.

Dear Father,

Thank you that I can draw near to you. I thank you that I can now be filled with your Holy Spirit. I realize that I can do nothing by myself to fight these demons, so I am claiming the authority of Jesus Christ who lives inside of me. I claim your promise that the blood of Christ gives me great power over demonic attacks. Father, I thank you that I can resist Satan and his demonic helpers and they will flee because Jesus lives in me and is far greater than the devil and all his forces. And so, in the name of Jesus I am now commanding these evil spirits to leave and never return. In Jesus' name, Amen.

Debbie, I want you to know that God loves you and that you are not alone. You need to make as many Christian friends as you can. Keep believing that in Christ's power victory is yours.

Your friend in the battle,
Dawson

9

We Do Have Hope

"I don't understand why God chose to present so many situations to me. . . . God must be planning one heck of a ministry for me."
—JoAnn

IT WOULD BE EASY TO LOOK AT ALL the different letters in this book and come to the conclusion that every student in America has deep problems and that there is no hope. But that is hardly the case. I receive hundreds of letters each year from students who, while facing difficultly, are trusting Christ. There are still tens of thousands of Christian students from strong homes who are relatively secure. They are being used for God. In fact, when I think about the American teenager, I am encouraged by several things. One is that many Christian students are coming to the conclusion that there is no middle ground in living for Christ. They are learning that unless you sell out for Christ, that is, unless you've given it your all, you will be pulled down by our sick and decadent world. And so they have decided to share their faith and live for Him.

I am also encouraged because today's Christian students are very knowledgeable about the emotional pain in their world. They are very much concerned about the struggles of their non-Christian friends, and they want to do something about their struggles. I believe today's students are more compassionate and prayerful than many students were thirty years ago.

A third encouraging sign is that today's Christian students seem to be growing through their own pain. Even though many of them have been hurt while growing up, they have allowed God to begin healing them and, in the process, using them. It reminds me of a verse in Romans:

But when sin grew worse, God's grace increased.

Romans 5:20b

God has stepped in to help these hurting teenagers find peace in Him and work through the struggles they are facing. This gives me hope. There is a new wave of Christian students who are rising up to live for God and tell another generation about Christ.

There is one more letter I want to share with you. It's from JoAnn. I believe it illustrates the new kind of Christian student I have just discussed. Here is a girl who has come from a bad home, has a difficult physical situation, and is being laughed at by her peers. Yet in spite of it all, this determined girl is trusting Christ. She is a living illustration of God's promise in Jeremiah 29.

"I say this because I know what I am planning for you," says the LORD. "I have good plans for you, not plans to hurt you. I will give you hope and a good future."

Jeremiah 29:11

If there were ever a verse that sums up how God feels about our teenagers as they approach the twenty-first century, this is it. I want to issue a challenge to every person who is reading these words right now: God has not given up on the American teenager, and we shouldn't either. God offers hope to hurting kids, and so should we. I trust JoAnn's letter will encourage you as it did me.

A Letter from JoAnn

Dear Dawson,

I couldn't help but write you after listening to your radio program tonight. I didn't even know our radio station started carrying your program. I wrote to you a long time ago at your last conference. I left a note on your podium and you read it and wrote me back. My life was touched. I don't know if you remember, but I don't live with my family because my mom's boyfriend was abusing me sexually. The state took me away from my house and I haven't been back since. I've been living in a foster group home. I'm eighteen and a senior, but I'm allowed to stay here until I graduate. Anyway, since I've been here the Lord has helped me considerably. He has allowed me to get help for my problems. Dawson, I have a severe case of scoliosis. The doctors performed a spinal fusion. This leveled the hump on my back and allowed my severe upper curve to chill out.

Since they took my rods out the hump on my back has increased. The hump is caused by my ribs moving due to my curve. I take an incredible 'razzing' from the kids in school. I get punched on, laughed at, and talked down on. Just because I look different people think I'm mentally retarded. They talk loud and slow. Dawson, I'm not stupid. In fact, God has given me many talents.

I'm just struggling with a lot of things at once. My real mom is still causing me heartache. She told me when I was seventeen that she couldn't wait for me to be eighteen so we could start doing things as a family, including Bob, the guy who abused me. I was excited because in August I'll be leaving for college and I want to spend as much time with my little brother and the family as I can. I've forgiven the guy who abused me, and if my mom is planning to marry, sooner or later we'll come face to face.

Dawson, I love my little brother a lot, but it seems like he's afraid of me. He's eleven and very aggressive, and when I ask about home he says that my mommy told him to be quiet. I feel like I'm losing him too. I already lost my older brother. I don't understand why God chose to present so many situations to me, but I ask that you help me out the best you can.

Dawson, the most exciting thing about all this that is going on is God must be planning one heck of a ministry for me. He already has given me an excellent testimony.

Dawson, I'll write again on the ninth because that is when I find out what the doctor's found in the EMG and MRI tests I had done. I'm very nervous. . . .

Well thanks for listening.

Love in Christ,
JoAnn

P.S. Keep up the great work on your radio show!

Dear JoAnn,

I have read your letter, and I can't begin to tell you how much it has encouraged me. You see, I get hundreds and hundreds of letters from teenagers all over America. Most of these letters, like yours, are filled with plenty of heartbreak. However, while many of the students I hear from seem stuck in their problems, you are fighting back. In spite of all your hard times, you have chosen to rely on God. Your determination to trust the Lord to solve your problems is truly remarkable. I am very proud of you. Through Christ, you are winning a tremendous victory.

I want you to know that I am really sorry that you were sexually abused. I know that what your mother's boyfriend did to you has caused you a lot of suffering. It's too bad that your mother doesn't understand that you had to come forward and tell the truth. I am praying that, in time, she will see so much of Jesus in you that she will turn away from her own sin and rebellion and get right with God. Nevertheless, I am thrilled that God has given you the grace and the power to forgive this man. I am also encouraged that you are in a good foster-group home. God is clearly showing you His love by taking care of you and meeting your needs. I hope you realize that, just as God has been faithful to you in the past, He will continue to take care of you in the future. In fact, here are some verses from Psalm 46 that I want you to memorize.

God is our protection and our strength. He always helps in times of trouble. So we will not be afraid if the earth shakes, or if the mountains fall into the sea, even if the oceans roar and foam, or the mountains shake at the raging sea.
Psalm 46:1–3

JoAnn, these verses are just as true today as when King David wrote them. God is completely committed to loving and protecting you no matter what may come your way. You've done great so far. Keep trusting Him.

I was deeply moved when you told me about the

problems you are having with the hump on your back.
When I read that section of your letter I found myself
sad, angry, and touched, all at the same time. The way
other teenagers tease and laugh at you breaks my heart.
One day they will need compassion. On that day, I hope
they remember you. I am sad for those people who treat
you like you are mentally retarded. They are afraid to
take the time to really get to know you. It is their loss.
But the thought that came to my mind is that your
situation seems very similar to one faced by Jesus Himself. He wasn't really very good looking. There was
nothing in His appearance that would make people
want to come to Him. In fact, there were people who
looked the other way when they saw Him. In Isaiah 53,
the Bible not only tells us about Christ's physical appearance, but also predicted some of the terrible abuse
He would face.

> **He grew up like a small plant before the
> Lord, like a root growing in a dry land. He had no
> special beauty or form to make us notice him;
> there was nothing in his appearance to make us
> desire him. He was hated and rejected by people.
> He had much pain and suffering. People would
> not even look at him. He was hated, and we didn't
> even notice him.**
>
> Isaiah 53:2–3

Jesus took horrible abuse from cruel and hateful
people. You know it had to hurt Him. Isaiah called
Him a man who "had much pain and suffering." Yet
God chose Him to shake the world for all eternity. Was
it because He was good looking or acceptable to the

popular people? No. Jesus was greatly used by God because He totally trusted the Father, even when everyone turned against Him. JoAnn, God is using you too. It's not because you're outwardly beautiful or accepted by most of the kids in your school. God is using you because, in spite of all the pain you have been through, you still trust and love Him.

I think it's hard for all of us to understand why God allows pain and suffering in our lives. And unfortunately, you have had to go through far more than most people your age. But I think these verses in 2 Corinthians help us all to realize what God has in mind when He allows our troubles.

> **We have small troubles for a while now, but they are helping us gain an eternal glory that is much greater than the troubles. We set our eyes not on what we see but on what we cannot see. What we see will last only a short time, but what we cannot see will last forever.**
>
> **2 Corinthians 4:17–18**

Think of it, JoAnn; God is allowing your problems not because He wants you to suffer, but because He knows they are helping you receive huge rewards in heaven. Compared to all eternity, your troubles are really small, but the rewards ahead of you are so great that you and I cannot even comprehend them. Do you know the best part of this? Every day you trust God through your struggles, your heavenly rewards grow bigger and bigger. I think when we get to heaven and God starts giving out rewards, some fairly well-known Christians will be way at the back of the line. But you and others who have trusted God through much pain and injustice will be at the front of the line receiving huge rewards.

No, JoAnn, you're certainly not stupid. And yes, JoAnn, God has given you many talents. I believe you can accomplish anything you set your mind to do. And I am sure you are right, JoAnn, God must be planning "one heck of a ministry" for you. You have already come through more trials than some Christians ever face. And finally, JoAnn, I agree with all my heart when you say, "He already has given me an excellent testimony." Your testimony has touched me very deeply, and I want to thank you for it. You truly are a joy to God. Hang in there and keep up the good work.

> Proud to be your friend,
> Dawson

Need Help?

If you are age twenty-one or younger and in need of counseling, call our Hope Line,

1-800-394-HOPE

during the following hours: Sunday night between 7:00 and 10:00 CST or between 3:00 and 6:00 P.M. CST Monday through Thursday.

or write to us at:

Dawson McAllister
PO Box 3512
Irving, TX 75015

If you would like additional resources from Dawson McAllister and others, or would like to know about the Dawson McAllister Student Conferences in your area, write or call:

Shepherd Ministries
2845 W. Airport Freeway,
Suite 137
Irving, TX 75062
1–214–570–7599
Fax 214–257–0632

Also available from Shepherd: student and teacher manuals about such topics as self-esteem, peer and family relationships, as well as teaching and contemporary Christian music videos and tapes.